Cyber Terrorism:
Political and Economic Implications

Andrew Michael Colarik

IDEA GROUP PUBLISHING
Hershey • London • Melbourne • Singapore

Acquisitions Editor:	Michelle Potter
Development Editor:	Kristin Roth
Senior Managing Editor:	Amanda Appicello
Managing Editor:	Jennifer Neidig
Copy Editor:	Angela Thor
Typesetter:	Sharon Berger
Cover Design:	Lisa Tosheff
Printed at:	Integrated Book Technology

Published in the United States of America by
Idea Group Publishing (an imprint of Idea Group Inc.)
701 E. Chocolate Avenue
Hershey PA 17033
Tel: 717-533-8845
Fax: 717-533-8661
E-mail: cust@idea-group.com
Web site: http://www.idea-group.com

and in the United Kingdom by
Idea Group Publishing (an imprint of Idea Group Inc.)
3 Henrietta Street
Covent Garden
London WC2E 8LU
Tel: 44 20 7240 0856
Fax: 44 20 7379 0609
Web site: http://www.eurospanonline.com

Library of Congress Cataloging-in-Publication Data

Colarik, Andrew M.
  Cyber terrorism : political and economic implications / Andrew M. Colarik.
     p. cm.
  Summary: "This book is a brief that outlines many of the recent terrorist activities, political objectives, and their use of cyber space"--Provided by publisher.
  Includes bibliographical references and index.
  ISBN 1-59904-021-2 (hardcover) -- ISBN 1-59904-022-0 (soft cover) -- ISBN 1-59904-023-9 (ebook)
  1. Cyberterrorism. 2. Computer crimes. 3. Information superhighway--Economic aspects. 4. Information warfare--Political aspects. 5. Asymmetric warfare. 6. Computer networks--Security measures. I. Title: Cyberterrorism : political and economic implications. II. Title.

HV6773.C64 2006
363.325--dc22

                                                                    2005034831

British Cataloguing in Publication Data
A Cataloguing in Publication record for this book is available from the British Library.

How do you pick up the threads of an old life?
How do you go on,
when in your heart you begin to understand.
There is no going back.

- Frodo Baggins

Cyber Terrorism:
Political and Economic Implications

Table of Contents

Chapter V

Current Cyber Attack Methods **82**

Chapter VI

Attack Scenarios **111**

Foreword

Computing began its existence as a novelty in the 1930s with Konrad Zuse's *Z-1*, became a strategic weapon in the 1940s with Tommy Flowers and Max Newman's *Colossus*, and from the 1950s onward, a tool of business. We have seen its capabilities and use, evolve through batch processing and time sharing, to online real-time processing. The means of communicating with these was via direct wiring through dumb and smart terminals, and eventually via a network through personal computers.

Personal computers evolved in parallel, with the 1950 novelty *Simple Simon*, through the 1970s, with the developments of *Altair* and others who provided a gaming capability for home players, and through the 1980s, when the personal computer came into its own as a business tool.

Networking, as we know it, really began in 1969 with the creation of *ARPANet* and the connection of the four original players (UCLA connected September, Stanford Research Institute connected October, University of California at Santa Barbara connected November, University of Utah connected December). It was originally designed to be a fault tolerant network with the primary imperative of reliability at its heart. ARPANet was never designed to be secure or to be used for business. The *Internet* too has evolved from its early beginnings as ARPANet, over the years, to become the world network which links the people of every country. Trillions of dollars of business are transacted over the Internet. Strategic activities are directed by the use of the Internet as the main means of communications. Utilities and public services are controlled via the Internet.

The power of computing has increased exponentially in concert with the reducing costs until today: computers are now ubiquitous. The linkage of this technology with the *Internet* has made it possible for easy inexpensive communication throughout the world. The availability of computers has made it possible for millions of people to gain differing levels of expertise that were impossible before. The positive result is that this technology serves humanity in ways that no other has ever in the past. This service has resulted in reliance on its use beyond anyone's wildest expectations. The global information infrastructure has become vital to economies all over the world: so much so that it presents itself as a primary target to terrorists and extortionists alike the world over.

Andrew Colarik's book is a timely and important work that addresses the implications of this dependence. Exploding a bomb can cause a huge effect, but it costs a great deal to create and deliver. Conducting a computerized attack can be just as disruptive (or more so), but costs practically nothing to implement. *Cyber terrorism* looks at how attacking the Internet, and those connected, becomes a force multiplier for those with an agenda, whatever that might be.

The evolution of cyber-attack methods gives the reader an understanding of where hacking began and how it has, and continues, to develop. We can expect that there will be new attacks, and that committed people will find ways to use these techniques to further their respective agendas. It is also apparent that they can magnify the damage caused by distributing these strategies to others, who will experiment with them and use them too.

The relative breadth of potential targets is addressed. The reader may be as surprised as I was to learn of the many different and all pervasive systems and networks that could be damaged or destroyed, all of which would negatively affect those who depend on the services provided by them.

It is interesting to have a look at the various attack methods that have been identified and documented. To be sure, there will be others, yet unknown, to come. However, a pattern begins to unfold that is borne out by the evolution of these. That pattern is that the global information infrastructure is insecure.

The events in New York in 2001 have begun to bring home the idea that we must protect the vital functions provided by the Internet and those connected. Andrew's book highlights the notion that we must better protect the global information infrastructure, demonstrating why we must be prepared for the consequences of new attack strategies.

Cyber Terrorism: Political and Economic Implications is a reference that every executive should have read first, and then passed on to their subordinates for them to read as well. The only way that the battle against this kind of terrorism will be won is by education that not only covers organizational management and the technicians within who are responsible for information technology, but also the software and hardware providers. With a concerted effort and commitment from all of us, the global information infrastructure can be made safe from terrorists.

Dr. Henry B. Wolfe
University of Otago
October 2005

Henry B. Wolfe, PhD, has been an active computer professional for 45 years. He has earned a number of university degrees, culminating with a Doctor of Philosophy from the University of Otago (virus defenses in the MS/DOS environment). The first 10 years of his career were spent designing systems in the manufacturing environment; the most notable was one of the first fully-automated accounting systems in the U.S. The next 10 years of ever-increasing responsibility was devoted to serving in the U.S. Federal Government, rising to the position of director of management information systems for the Overseas Private Investment Corporation.

In 1979, Dr. Wolfe took up an academic post at the University of Otago, and for the past 20 or so years, has specialized in computer security (creating one of the first of the few security curriculum in the southern hemisphere). During that period, he has earned an international reputation in the field of forensics, encryption, surveillance, privacy, and computer virus defenses.

He has provided advice on security matters to major government bodies within New Zealand, and to Australian, Panamanian, Singaporean and U.S. government organizations, and additionally to New Zealand businesses and the major New Zealand Internet service providers.

Preface

In today's world, we are becoming more connected by communications and information technologies than ever before. Telecommunication systems and computers have global reach, transmitting voice and data digitally across transnational borders. These systems support economic infrastructures such as the energy and transportation industries, as well as all kinds of commerce and governmental services. This global information infrastructure is the principle foundation for the current integration of economies, cultures, and societies that is taking place throughout the world. It allows for the free flow of thoughts, ideas, and life-changing events that are used in instilling a greater sense of freedom and open democratic processes to people around the world. Never before has there been so much access to so much information that is available in a moments notice. These prolific capabilities have not gone unnoticed by developed countries, nor have they failed to harness their economic benefits as a competitive advantage. They have also not gone unnoticed by Western adversaries.

Information systems technologies are being used to make our lives more efficient. Scales of economies are gained when inefficiencies and redundancies can be reduced through the proper application of information technology. However, such efficiencies have their consequences. Every day we depend more and more on interconnected systems such as telecommunications; electronic banking; global stock markets; international traffic systems; water supply purification and distribution systems; electrical, gas, and nuclear power production and distribution; radio and television; emergency services; and the list goes on. All of these infrastructures utilize information systems to manage and distribute their services, and are the basis for creating large-scale economic efficiencies in modern societies. By creating and maintaining reliable core infrastructures, a society may then devote its energies towards higher levels of efficient production, further development of innovation, and progressive thought. When this is not the case, significant effort and resources are instead deployed to continual damage control and repair, and as such, further development is greatly diminished. In a paper written for the First Committee on Disarmament and International Security (UNISCA) in December of 2002, Jonas Böttler, from the Delegation of Canada, stated "The more developed a country is, the more it depends on the correct and safe work of all these systems. Any intrusion, manipulation, sabotage, disruption or even destruction on one of these networks or systems will have effects which go far beyond the affection of only the attacked system itself." Therefore, in order for developed societies to maintain their economic superiority, they must secure their underlying infrastructures. When vulnerability does exist, history has shown that competing forces will surely use it to their advantage and their opponent's disadvantage. It is for this reason that this book was written.

People and systems are vulnerable to the methods and processes they employ to get things done. This is because they learn to trust their underlying successes and apply this trust to future applications of their approach. There is a clear link between the elimination of trust and the instillment of fear. It has been proposed that the attacks of September 11th in 2001 (i.e., when the World Trade Towers were destroyed, the Pentagon was damaged, the flight over Pennsylvania was downed, and thousands perished) occurred as a result of asymmetric thinking on the part of the terrorist group al Qaeda. When an opponent is attacked at right angles to their traditional thinking methods, they become vulnerable and unprepared for what is to come. This is known as asymmetric warfare, and is becoming a terrorist's first choice of attack, given the opportunity. The use of jetliners as missiles never occurred to the passengers and civil defense authorities alike until it was too late. It was simply unimaginable, and this notion has played a significant role in traumatizing many who watched these horrific images. The application of the traditional applied in a radically nontraditional manner both seems to be unimaginable and frighteningly real when it happens, especially when it comes to technology. Those with the capability of asymmetric thinking have unforetold power to change and shape the future directly and indirectly through their actions. It is asymmetric thinking applied to technology that has become the countervailing power to the global information infrastructure's ability to enact social, cultural, and economic change.

Historically, power comes in many forms. It may be acquired through position, such as being the head of an organization. Power may be acquired through the application of someone's personality, such as charisma and leadership qualities. But ultimately, power is the ability to take action by employing position, personality, and the control of resources. With respect to terrorists and those combating terrorism, the amount of power through action is dependent on three basic factors. The first of these is knowledge of ones self, including ones abilities and short comings. For without such insights, any action taken may result in limited success, which may not be capable of being sustained. The second is knowledge of one's opponent, which includes their methods, strengths, and weaknesses. Doing battle without first understanding the capabilities of an opponent is reckless at best, and could be fatal at worst. The third is the control and application of resources that can amplify and focus one's abilities to act and/or compensate for one's shortcomings in taking action. Because westernized countries have such economic might, large amounts of resources can be brought to bear as a force amplifier while lessening any shortsightedness, or a lack of inherent aptitudes when confronting adversaries. This author leaves it to the reader to judge the political and military activities of their own respective countries. However, conflict between competing forces and the desire to have power over them is as old as civilization itself. The desire to grow stronger and create a more powerful position to enact change is ever present in an evolving world.

The adversaries that Western nations now face have shown a great aptitude and patience for developing their member's understanding of themselves through education, military, and religious rigors. They have demonstrated a desire to learn about their targets by studying their culture and methods while living amongst them. Many of the hijackers in the September 11th attacks had lived and studied in several Western countries in Europe and North America. In fact, many held advanced degrees in a range of technologies. These terrorists have demonstrated that they can now use our own knowledge and technology against us to create largescale damage using relatively small amounts of resources, and in doing so, turn our own methods and approaches against us. The real question at hand is what can we do to stop them?

It has been said that information is power. Information is one of the West's greatest strengths. We rely on it as a primary foundation for supporting our open, democratic processes. The dissemination of information provides citizens of democratic countries with the ability to stay informed about their government's activities (good and bad), and to make decisions on a collective basis for their own respective well-being and sustained futures. Accurate and timely information provides a distinct competitive advantage in all aspects of living and governance. Information is, in fact, a commodity unto itself, as it is regularly packaged, traded, and sold around the globe, affecting monetary and commercial markets. As previously mentioned, the use of technologies that facilitate the sharing of information, societies, and economies are becoming closer, more familiar, and increasingly integrated, as their exposure to each other occurs more and more each day. As such, the global information infrastructure is both a tool for furthering Western ideals and ideologies, and is a facilitator and target for those forces seeking to diminish its influence and progress. Therefore, our reliance on the mechanisms, systems, and basic infrastructures that support the use of information is both subject to being used for violence, as well as being a target of violence. Everyday technologies used by hundreds of millions of people are now a new tool in the arsenal of terrorists, and this form of terrorism is known as cyber terrorism.

In the 1980s, it has been reported that the term cyber terrorism was defined by Barry Collin to represent the convergence of cyberspace and terrorism. Since that time, the term has continued to change in definition, and has had its scope expanded to the point where it has become a wholly subjective term that has lost its true focus (i.e., where true terror and cyberspace converge). Other prominent authors and governmental actors have offered their definitions, but most have lost the core connection to terrorism itself, and have instead disconnected the electronic world from the physical world. In fact, the term "terrorism" has been hijacked by self-interests seeking an expansion of their respective controls and power base by turning this term into a form of *fearism*. This book seeks to establish cyber terrorism as it is applied to the global information infrastructure and its use by terrorists for the creation of violence and not just fear. It has become commonplace to label an aggressive, nonviolent act as a form of terrorism, just as it has become commonplace for a major computer disruption to be labeled as an act of cyber terrorism. Such approaches diminish our ability to enact effective security measures and instill mature responses when such true terrorism occurs. With over 20 years of definitions, discussions, and debates over what cyber terrorism is and what we should do about it, it is now here and affects us all. It is now time to create a real awareness of the threat of cyber terrorism so we can mobilize and focus our efforts in creating a safer world dependent on using information technology.

The notion that terrorists are ignorant and unskilled needs to change. With the proliferation of the Internet, global reach by terrorists to potential target intelligence, and its dissemination amongst their members and affiliated groups is now possible in near real time. This usage with the acquisition of additional skills affords them the opportunity to master the underlying technologies and infrastructures that may ultimately be used to cripple our own information infrastructure and facilitate future physical attacks against us. Accessing critical information remotely is but the tip of the iceberg. Because we rely on these systems to control utilities, govern financial institutions, utilize medical databases for healthcare, and logistical support for military operations, terrorists can institute widespread chaos as well as precision targeting through a host of technology-driven attack methods. These new technologically skilled terrorists are providing the information and communication support for terrorist operations. As their skills continue to increase (and they will), cyber terrorists will commence assaults on high-value targets through the interception of confidential communications, the modification of critical data resulting in physical harm, and the denial of resources in times of crisis used in conjunction with physical attacks.

This emerging domain will affect everyone as we are forced to change how we utilize surveillance techniques and apply personal countersurveillance techniques to everyday activities. Because terrorist groups such as al Qaeda have demonstrated that they are capable of thinking outside our mental boxes, the weapon of choice by the majority of governments and individuals must be good intelligence (i.e., information) on terrorist activities in order to prevent future attacks and preparing ourselves for any resulting consequences of such attacks. Privacy issues and the rights of individuals to self-govern their information will emerge as a result of poor intelligence and counterintelligence measures. In fact, if governments and organizations misapply these technologies, they may actually cause sympathy for those labeled as terrorists. It is this author's sincerest belief that if left unchecked, cyber terrorism will become the principle motivator for creating a culture of security in the Information Age. This book was written to help create an awareness of the problem, and its primary contributions to the domain of cyber terrorism consist of:

- The role of information technology in terrorism (Chapter I),
- Identifies the various forms of traditional terrorism taking place in today's world as a foundation for its broad usage of cyberspace (Chapter II),
- Outlines and identifies a simple progression from hacker, cracker, cyber criminal to cyber terrorist (Chapter III),
- Offers a focused definition of cyber terrorism that is strongly attached to terrorism (Chapter III),

- Identifies the foundational components of the global information infrastructure and many of its core security services, mechanisms, and protocols (Chapter IV),
- Pinpoints many of the current modes of electronic attack and corresponding vulnerabilities (Chapter V),
- Puts forward a host of attack scenarios for key economic sectors and individuals (Chapter VI), and
- Proposes simple, preventative ideas designed to resolve many of the core issues to securing the global information infrastructure from cyber terrorists and cyber criminals alike (Chapter VII).

In short, it is the usage of technology, and in particular the global information infrastructure, by which terrorists communicate, coordinate, and facilitate their initiatives, that this book addresses. It is a *brief*, designed to provide an overview of terrorist activities, and their evolving use of information technologies. This book also provides the needed simplified details of our dependence on information systems to begin a common dialog between all stakeholders for creating rational initiatives. Finally, this book aims to propose ideas that address many of the larger issues governing the protection of data and information, rather than detailed solutions to any particular security area.

Acknowledgments

I would like to thank everyone who helped to bring this book project to a conclusion. It is amazing to me all the personal support for this topic that exists amongst the good people I have encountered. I would also like to thank everyone in advance who helps distribute this book in order to build an awareness of the importance of the emerging domain of cyber terrorism. Hopefully, a proactive approach to securing the global information infrastructure may help to prevent future disasters in the making. May God's blessings be upon you, your family, and all your efforts in creating a safer world.

Chapter I

Introduction

Objectives of This Chapter

√   Learn more about recent terrorist atrocities.

√   Identify the main sponsors of global terrorism today.

√   Comprehend the link between diminished terrorist attacks over time and their need to create new venues/methods of global reach and devastation.

√   Understand the organizational link between terrorists and technology.

√   Begin to discover the importance of securing the global information infrastructure.

Terrorist Atrocities

Over the past decade, armed conflicts have occurred all over the world. In Algeria, Islamic groups have attacked key economic targets, officials, and foreigners. In Egypt, the Muslim Brotherhood waged an insurgent's war that has evolved to political participation as a direct result of a series of armed defeats by the government. Ongoing independence efforts by Indonesian islands, as well as religious conflicts between Christians and Muslims within Indonesia, continue to escalate. The most recent result in Indonesia is East Timor, newly formed in 1999 after many bloody conflicts resulting in high loss of life. India and Pakistan have been warring in Kashmir, and have nearly gone to nuclear war several times over this disputed region. As a result of Sharia law being implemented in Nigeria, violent clashes between Christians and Muslims continue to escalate. Last of these is the Israeli and Palestinian conflict, which has spawned a host of wars, bombings, and so-called regionalized violence that has been used to justify violence movements around the globe.

The most notable and horrific of these attacks in recent history was when al Qaeda hijackers flew jetliners into the World Trade Center towers, the Pentagon, and crashed a fourth plane in a Pennsylvania field, killing nearly 3,000 people in total and causing untold economic, political, and social damages. This single event on September 11th in 2001 triggered the War on Terror campaign, resulting in the removal of Taliban rule in Afghanistan, as well as a major shift in interventionist policies.

In 2002, terrorists continued their assaults on Western targets. The nightclub bombings in Bali, Indonesia by Jemaah Islamiyah (a group linked to al Qaeda) killed more than 180 people. In the same year, Chechen rebels held a Moscow theater, with hundreds of hostages in it, for 3 days. During efforts to rescue said hostages, more than 100 people were killed from the incapacitating gas used in the rescue. In Istanbul, Turkey, suicide bombers attacked the British consulate, an HSBC bank, and several synagogues, resulting in the injuring of hundreds and the deaths of more than 60 people. Those terrorist groups claiming responsibility are reported to have links to al Qaeda.

According to the U.S. State Department, in 2003, attacks occurred in Afghanistan, Algeria, Belgium, Chile, Columbia, Cuba, France, Greece, the Gaza Strip, India, Indonesia, Iraq, Israel, Italy, Jordan, Kenya, Kuwait, Lebanon, Malaysia, Morocco, Pakistan, Panama, Peru, Philippines, Saudi Arabia, Serbia, Somalia, Spain, Turkey, Venezuela, and the West Bank. These included everything from kidnappings, bombings, hijackings, politically motivated murders, and nerve agent attacks.

In 2004, a bomb planted by an operative of Abu Sayyaf (an al Qaeda-linked group) exploded, sinking a ferry in Manila Bay in the Philippines, which left 116 people dead or missing. In Madrid, Spain, coordinated explosions at three train stations killed more than 190 people. Authorities suspect Amer el-Azizi as the mastermind, who has also been indicted in Spain for the September 11th attacks. In Russia, 200 people, including children, were killed when at least 30 heavily armed hostage takers took over a school. The deaths occurred when authorities attempted to end the standoff and the terrorists open fired on the hostages.

In 2005, three coordinated suicide bomb attacks exploded in London's subway system during morning rush hour, and coincided with the 31st G8 Summit being held in Scotland. These attacks resulted in the deaths of 56 people and over 700 injured. Two weeks later, another set of bombing attacks occurred in the same transit system. These botched follow-up attacks resulted in no direct injuries, numerous arrests, and widespread media coverage. In Bali, Indonesia a suicide bomber killed 25 and injured another 90 in a restaurant. The attack is reported to be the work of the al Qaeda linked group Jemaah Islamiah (JI). Such attacks are designed to create lasting fear in the day-to-day activities of our daily lives.

The world is not always a safe place to live, and these types of violence are not restricted to distant lands. Nor are they only committed by so-called revolutionaries and religious zealots. Despite these decrepit acts, it should be noted that the occurrences and frequencies of terrorist attacks are actually diminishing, while the media's coverage of such events continues to rise. The ongoing antiterrorist activities of most governments continue to be the cause for the reductions. Additional reasons for the decline will be discussed in later sections and chapters.

State Sponsors of Terror

States that sponsor terrorism take advantage of deniability. This long-standing tradition has been an effective means for antagonizing perceived enemies and more powerful adversaries, while showing no active participation in any direct attacks. Through providing training, logistical support, intelligence, and funds, insurgences can be created that diminish the social and economic efforts of maintaining a stable regime, as well as a growing economy.

When insurgents strike at their targets, they may suffer losses and retreat in order to fight another day. In many cases, simply by providing shelter and so-called humanitarian support, state sponsors can provide the time needed to reconstitute a terrorist organization's reorganization, so that it may sustain losses and recover from setbacks to come back stronger than before. This asylum assistance in turn creates additional social-political support by minority or repressed peoples to support so-called freedom fighters with the legitimacy of state sponsorships, such as in the case of Lebanon's hosting of the Palestinian Liberation Organization (PLO) in 1971. As continued activities by the sponsored group become elevated in the public light, state sponsorships may eventually lead to legitimacy, as is the case when a proclamation by Arab states at the Rabat Conference occurred, stating that the PLO was the sole, legitimate representative of the Palestinian people (Brynen, 1990).

State sponsorship of terrorism continues today. The U.S. State Department reported in 2003 that Cuba, Iran, North Korea, and Syria continued to show little change in their positions regarding state sponsorship of terrorism. The report goes on to state:

- *Cuba remained opposed to the US-led Coalition prosecuting the global war on terrorism and continued to provide support to designated foreign terrorist organizations and to host several terrorists and dozens of fugitives from US state and federal justice. Cuba allowed Basque Fatherland and Liberty (ETA) members to reside in the country and provided support and safe haven to members of the Colombian Revolutionary Armed Forces (FARC) and the National Liberation Army (ELN).*

- *Iran remained the most active state sponsor of terrorism in 2003: Islamic Revolutionary Guard and Ministry of Intelligence and Security personnel were involved in planning and support for terrorist acts. Although Iran detained al Qaeda operatives in 2003, it refused to identify senior members in custody. Tehran continued to encourage anti-Israel activities, both operationally and rhetorically, providing logistic support and training to Lebanese Hizballah and a variety of Palestinian rejectionist groups.*

- *North Korea announced it planned to sign several antiterrorism conventions but did not take any substantive steps to cooperate in efforts to combat terrorism.*

- *Syria continued to provide support to Palestinian rejectionist groups and allowed them to operate out of Syria, albeit with a lower profile after May 2003. Syria also served as a transshipment point for Iranian supply of Hizballah in Lebanon, and although Syrian officials have publicly condemned terrorism, they continue to distinguish between terrorism and what they view as legitimate resistance against Israel.*

Other countries have participated in the state sponsorship of terror for decades, and in some cases, for centuries. However, the U.S. government's interventionist policies regarding the War on Terror has given many regimes pause for thought, especially when the subsequent removal of Saddam Hussain's regime in Iraq occurred, despite the fact that many countries and citizens were against such an action. As a result, new diplomatic avenues with previously established state-sponsored terrorism states are occurring on a global basis. The short-term perspective of these states is changing and being mitigated as to the outcomes of sponsorships. For many regimes, today's terrorist attacks are no longer being considered a cost of doing business in order to pacify minority religious and political interests, because of the disruptive capabilities that now exist.

Frequency of Attacks

The number of attacks by terrorist organizations has actually decreased over the last several decades, with momentary spikes every 4 to 5 years (see Figure 1). This is primarily because of organized efforts by the G-8 (i.e., Canada, France, Germany, Italy, Japan, Russia, the United Kingdom, and the United States), members of the United Nations Security Council, and vested government and commercial interests to reduce such threats in order to continue the expansion of the globalization of social, economic, and political relations. It is these growing ties that terrorists seek to diminish, disrupt, and ultimately destroy in order to pursue their respective agendas. Because some governments have shown the willingness to pursue terrorists on a collective level, and

Figure 1. U.S. State Department reporting of international terrorist attacks

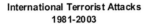

**International Terrorist Attacks
1981-2003**

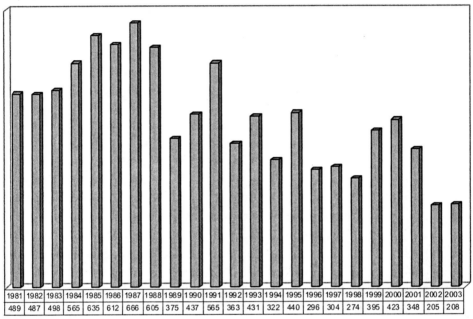

1981	1982	1983	1984	1985	1986	1987	1988	1989	1990	1991	1992	1993	1994	1995	1996	1997	1998	1999	2000	2001	2002	2003
489	487	498	565	635	612	666	605	375	437	565	363	431	322	440	296	304	274	395	423	348	205	208

Attacks by Year

many more have now increased participation in eliminating terrorist threats, terrorists are now willing to escalate their destructive force and potential damages by utilizing weapons that have a higher casualty rate or dramatic outcome, while focusing on high value and/or symbolic targets (i.e., weapons of mass destruction, civilian infrastructure centers, etc.).

With the exception of the September 11th attacks and the London bombings, most attacks have resulted in perhaps several hundred people or less being injured and/or murdered. However, with the increased awareness and unprecedented cooperation taking place around the world to eliminate such attacks, the pressure for terrorists to produce ever increasing dramatic and effective results from their attacks are forcing terrorists and their state sponsors to seek more powerful weapons of destruction. Where these terrorist organizations cannot bring to bare their full destructive force, they may try to force a government to overreact to their threats. When a government institutes measures that appear tyrannical and oppressive in a manner that reduces or eliminates established civil liberties, such action swells the ranks of sympathizers and supporters of terrorist causes. Such sympathy drives financial and political support, and self-justifies their initial assaults and destructive actions. The mere threat of a devastating attack can have a profound impact on modern societies and economies alike.

Despite all the rhetoric coming from governments and terrorists alike, violence is being rationalized in an immoral manner. Violent attacks are often justified by governmentally labeled terrorists claiming to be that country's or religion's freedom fighter for a host of *reasons*. The fact of the matter is, the killing of innocent bystanders in opposition for a cause they have no direct contribution in is morally wrong. And yet, so-called righteous freedom fighters kill, maim, and injure the true innocent in our societies. This just cannot be justified, as freedom fighters do not kill children in their schools, attack humanitarian relief efforts, or take action to prevent the self-governing of a country by its own people. Unfortunately, it is the high visibility of these immoral acts that drives the use of terrorist violence. Historically, terrorists tend to attack high-profile targets for media visibility, key organizations and individuals that are moving towards open, self-governing rule, and critical infrastructures in order to disrupt the normal flow of everyday life. This approach is designed to cause enough fear and discomfort in society and its leadership that their demands, reasonable or not, are met because of pressures imposed by its citizens or subjects. Such tactics have, and will be with us for quite some time. The key issue at hand is in what form they may take.

The Role of Information and Technology

Before a premeditated response to terrorism can occur, a better understanding of the current modes of terrorist organizations and terrorist networks must be pursued. Terrorists are becoming more progressive and adaptive in their organizational structures and communications, and timely information plays a big role in just how effective an organization operates. Through utilizing the global information infrastructure and its underlying technologies, terrorists can operate in a virtual electronic world that provides them with numerous advantages for communication and coordination efforts, as well as assist in their ongoing development and expansion efforts. In the following sections, a discussion about these new capabilities and the resulting core issues will be presented.

Network Approach by Terrorist Groups

The current incarnation of terrorist organizations tends to be more networked and ad hoc. A network structure allows individuals, groups, and organizations to flatten their lines of authority and control through the use of a web of communication technologies, much in the same way that virtual corporations operate. As a result, organizations can be more flexible and resilient due to functional independence with operationally coordinated efforts (Ahuja & Carley, 1999). Information is critical to the control and coordination of networked organizations, and as such, the flow of information through communication channels is both its greatest strength and its greatest weakness. Key individuals in network structures therefore become the gateways and gatekeepers for directives from higher authoritative individuals, and for the dissemination of intelligence, skills, documentation, and supply logistics throughout a terrorist organization and its affiliates.

Networked terrorist organizations therefore rely on information as a means of group cohesion. With regards to command and control, the lowest level of control is where information is disseminated to all participants with equal access to posted information and communications. Individuals may decide for themselves what is important and what needs to be acted upon, such as information provided by Web sites, newsgroups, and postings such as formally declared jihads and fatwas. The middle level of control operates in a configuration similar to a set of hubs, where lesser individuals have access only to one or two hubs, so that informational control can be exerted in the same way that a regional manager directs a small group of people that have limited access to the rest of the organization, but interact easily within their respective groups. The highest level of control is highly hierarchical with a clear chain of command. This is where an organization's strategy for cultivating sociopolitical movements, and the power to enact its long-term plans, is channeled down through its underlying infrastructure.

Technology is the driving force behind networked, terrorist-organizational structures today. With access to the global telecommunications network from nearly anywhere in the world, localized terrorist cells can transmit and receive coordination and specialty communications from the middle tier of control. They may also disseminate past activities and so-called accomplishments for recruitment and movement validation purposes. If a cell proves its capabilities and commitment, operational support information (such as tactical and construction training materials) may be passed downwards to emerging cells.

Because this structure is distributed, the loss of contact by one group does not inhibit the activities of the rest, even though it does diminish a potential resource to the entire collaboration effort. In order to combat such a structure, armed strikes against these types of groups must occur only after good intelligence is obtained, in order to deduce the affiliations and true command structure(s). As previously stated, middle- and upper-level operatives are the key to controlling a distributed terrorist organization, as well as dismantling it.

In an article published in *Forbes* by Lenzner and Vardi in 2004, it was stated that "al Qaeda previously has used the Net to circulate propaganda and communicate with operatives. The terror alert in August, detailing al Qaeda plans to attack financial institutions in New York and New Jersey, came after the arrest in Pakistan of Muhammad Naeem Noor Khan, a computer engineer. Elsewhere, Abu Anas al-Liby, one of al Qaeda's ranking computer experts, trained agents in computer surveillance techniques, according to testimony in 2001 in the Nairobi embassy bombing trial." The logical extrapolations of these insights mean not only are terrorist organizations using technology, they are learning to exploit its full potential. So how do you fight and defeat a network structure? In this author's opinion, a network structure is needed to defeat a network structure. As a result of the aforementioned understandings, information such as intelligence, training, and logistical support must be used to fight the use and exploitation of information technologies by terrorist organizations, and a network structure involving multinational collaborations amongst governments and interested parties can be used to fight a network structure like al Qaeda and its state sponsors. It takes little understanding to see that the world's telecommunications networks are both the source of today's terrorist organizations' structure and coordinated capabilities, and also are the first effective means for dismantling these organizations when used by coordinated governments and societal organizations. Terrorist organizations are learning, growing organisms. They understand that mastery of the underlying technologies that make them successful will allow them to self-perpetuate themselves as well as defeat the intelligence being gathered by the very governments hunting them. Mastery or extinction is their only choice.

Main Issue and Problem:
The Global Information Infrastructure

The global information infrastructure is the foundational components and systems that permit all sorts of digital data to be transmitted, exchanged, and utilized by computer systems and stakeholders on a global basis. It encompasses the telecommunications infrastructure, as well as all the services that are facilitated by it, such as voice; cable, satellite and other wireless mediums; and the Internet. Through the use of such a system, the world has been able to share thoughts, ideas, innovations, and belief systems in ways and at a speed that has never been possible before. So why is this a problem?

First, new ideas that can be instituted quickly tend to create change faster than people can adapt emotionally. The need to slow and control change comes from this emotional insecurity or underdeveloped understanding of change itself. Second, because we are now in the so-called Information Age, information, or more importantly access to useful information, is power. The power to change anything that was previously well established on a regional or global scale is but one well-received phrase away. It is this author's opinion that this has caused an even greater struggle to control the hearts and minds of the peoples of the world. Third, large-scale efficiencies in our socioeconomic systems have occurred as a result of the high connectivity of systems and people alike. This will be elaborated throughout future chapters. Fourth, such a system is distributed, and therefore managed by thousands of organizations and millions of individuals throughout the world. Governing and standardizing a system this vast is an evolutionary process that comes from continuous conflicts and collaborations. Fifth and last, securing such a system from criminals and terrorists alike, given the previous four items, could take a lifetime if no incentives are put forward. Cyber terrorism is one such incentive.

The use of this infrastructure by traditional terrorists has broad implications. They may use such a resource for intimidation; to facilitate political strife or economic gain, or to undermine an economy; assert demands for the creation of an independent state, and/or assist in the destabilization of regimes; as a distribution channel for media empowerment of their activities; and for the organization of minority solidarity and subgroup confederations. A technosavvy terrorist may use such an infrastructure for target intelligence, electronic attacks, and most likely both in conjunction with physical attacks to increase attack effectiveness and further the traditional goals of terrorist organizations. This causes a critical concern for those individuals, businesses, and governments that use it for communication and interaction, and will ultimately force changes to its daily and long-term operating environment. As a result, it is always better to take a proactive approach to securing this system, rather than a reactionary one after people and entities have been irreversibly harmed. To do this for the global information infrastructure requires leadership, direction, and focus for the creation of prevention, response, and resolution initiatives. One major weakness that this author has discovered in reviewing the literature on cyber terrorism is that this domain has lots of definitions, many opinions, and few tangible, practical ideas. Perhaps what is needed is a set of core, tangible goals for the rest of the security world to begin working towards. Perhaps what is needed are contributors to the domain of cyber terrorism who bring with them ideas for solving the core issues. In the following chapters, this book will attempt to make a contribution towards clarifying the domain of cyber terrorism, its impact on the global information infrastructure, an attempt at understanding the wider security and privacy issues, and put forth a number of initiatives that can help secure this infrastructure for everyone.

Organization of This Book

It is the issue of terrorism and its use of cyberspace that will be addressed throughout this book. First, an examination of the power of terrorism in its various forms and applications, at a domestic, international, and global perspective, will be presented. This is followed by what cyber terrorism consists of, and the evolution of computer hackers to this latest incarnation (i.e., a cyber terrorist). One domain in which a cyber terrorist resides is the global information infrastructure, and this will be examined. An essential tool in the prevention process is an investigation of any potential attack scenarios and attack methods that may be used for these ends. These will be offered, as well as some thoughts for the prevention, response, and future policies that need to be considered to combat cyber terrorism.

Final Thoughts of This Chapter

The previous sections illustrate the importance of addressing terrorism, and in particular, the foundational infrastructure of the emerging domain of cyber terrorism. Postindustrial societies, and in particular westernized countries, are dependent on their information system infrastructures for communications, coordination, and dissemination of daily operations at all levels. The disruption of information infrastructures has been the goal of many an economic and/or political opponent, and is now emerging as the next battleground for the so-called War on Terror, and terrorists alike. Competing countries and criminal syndicates have developed sophisticated, information warfare capabilities, and these capabilities may very well be transferred to terrorists via state sponsorships and/or criminal purchase. By building an awareness of this emerging threat, and proposing rational solutions that address the core issues, it is the hope of this author that we may yet prevent serious loss of life and/or diminished quality of life. The rest of this book is dedicated to this goal.

References

Ahuja, M., & Carley, K. (1999). Network structure in virtual organizations. *Organization Science, 10*(6).

Brynen, R. (1990). *Sanctuary and survival: The PLO in Lebanon*. Boulder, CO: Westview Press.

Lenzer, R., & Vardi, N. (2004). Terror Inc. *Forbes*.

U.S. Department of State. (2004, April). *Patterns of global terrorism 2003*.

Additional Readings

Ajami, F. (2004, November 1). Bin Laden on TV: Arabia's latest addiction. *Wall Street Journal*.

Chazan, G. (2004, August 30). Plane crash sites in Russia point to terror attack; Wreckage contains traces of explosives as inquiry focuses on two passengers. *Wall Street Journal*.

Cloud, D. (1998, September 15). Investigators in Tanzania clarify picture of bombing, but they downplay arrests. *Wall Street Journal*.

Cook, D. (2003). The recovery of radical Islam in the wake of the defeat of the Taliban. *Terrorism and Political Violence, 15*(1).

Cotton, J. (2003). Southeast Asia after 11 September. *Terrorism and Political Violence, 15*(1).

Hookway, J. (2004, May 4) Sinking of ferry in Philippines tied to terrorism;

Muslim convert working with militant organization confesses to planting bomb. *Wall Street Journal.*

Hussain, Z., & Solomon, J. (2004, August 19). Al Qaeda gaining new support; Amid crackdown in Pakistan, cells form among middle class. *Wall Street Journal.*

Jaffe, G., & Fields, G. (2000, October 18). Yemenis link two Saudis to attack on U.S. Navy ship — Washington is skeptical, citing need to conduct its own investigation. *Wall Street Journal.*

Johnson, K. (2005, February 14). Terrorist threat shifts as groups mutate and merge; Disparate radicals united to bomb Madrid trains, court documents reveal. *Wall Street Journal.*

Mapes, T., Wagstaff, J., & Hindryati, R. (2004, September 10). Jakarta bomb goes off at Australian Embassy; Attack linked to al Qaeda comes as two countries prepare for key elections. *Wall Street Journal.*

McInerney, T., & Vallely, P. (2004, September 8). Iran's power play. *Wall Street Journal.*

Policy Working Group. (2005). *Report of the policy working group on the United Nations and terrorism.* Retrieved from http://www.un.org/terrorism/a57273.htm

Pope, H. (2001, August 10). Palestinian suicide attack kills 15 in Jerusalem — Lunchtime blast moves Israel to new kind of reprisal; Sharon, Bush face test. *Wall Street Journal.*

Solomon, J., & Hindryati, R. (2002, November 11). Bali inquiry turns to movements by suspects around the region. *Wall Street Journal.*

Spring, T. (2004, September). Al Qaeda's tech traps, investigations, arrests highlight how technology aids and weakens terror network. *PC World.*

Tan, A. (2003). Southeast Asia as the "second front" in the war against terrorism: Evaluating the threat and responses. *Terrorism and Political Violence, 15*(2).

Tucker, D. (2005). *What's new about the new terrorism and how dangerous is it?* Retrieved from http://www.nps.navy.mil/ctiw/files/The%20New%20Terrorism.pdf

Chapter II

The Power of Terrorism

Objectives of This Chapter

√   Create a foundational understanding of traditional terrorism in order to apply its goals, methods, and means to cyber terrorism.

√   Identify the key elements that comprise the term terrorism.

√   Understand the political orientation of terrorism.

√   Become aware of many of terrorism's actors throughout the world.

√   Discern many of the goals of terrorist organizations.

What is Terrorism?

There is no cyber terrorism without terrorism, period. Without a foundational understanding of terrorism in its various structures and forms, one can never fully appreciate its full exploitation of cyberspace. The true power of terrorism is fear enacted through violence. "Terrorism is an act and must be defined as such" (Flemming & Stohl, 2000). It is the intentional act of inflicting fear in an individual, group, and/or society with the intent to influence a wider audience. It is said that there are two basic motivations in life: the pursuit of pleasure and the avoidance of pain. The focus of terrorism is to inflict such terror through violence as to make people do anything to avoid the possibility of future pain. In this respect, a form of control is exercised on unwilling participants.

In Title 22 of the United States Code (18 CFR Section 2656f(d)), terrorism is defined as:

> *The term 'terrorism' means premeditated, politically motivated violence perpetrated against non-combatant targets by subnational groups or clandestine agents, usually intended to influence an audience.*

If one looks closely at this definition, it can be recognized that the term "noncombatant" is applied to the term *target*. Terrorists view all people in a society within and without their borders as potential targets, and as such, do not distinguish between combatants and noncombatants. This can be best illustrated by Osama bin Laden's fatwa for the Declaration of the World Islamic Front for Jihad Against the Jews and Crusaders, which appeared in a British newspaper in 1998. The article included the following statement:

> *The ruling to kill the Americans and their allies — civilians and military — is an individual duty for every Muslim who can do it in any country in which it is possible to do it, in order to liberate the al-Aqsa Mosque and the holy mosque from their grip, and in order for their armies to move out of all the lands of Islam, defeated and unable to threaten any Muslim. This is in accordance with the words of Almighty God.* (World Islamic Front, 1998)

At first glance, this appears to be a religious declaration of war. From a Muslim's perspective, it very well may be. Many within and without Islam have labeled groups like al Qaeda as religious fundamentalists and extremists, for a host of social, economic, and political reasons. But bin Laden continues to be considered a hero by Muslims around the world, despite the fact that ongoing terrorism has caused extreme hardships due to military, political, societal, and economic ruin everywhere it takes place. It is this author's understanding that there are deeper, more elementary reasons for this support that move beyond simple declarations and religious dogma.

In a journal article entitled *The Psychological and Behavioural Basis of Islamic Fundamentalism* by Taylor and Horgan (2001), the authors state that religious fundamentalism refers to the maintenance of traditional beliefs through a literal acceptance of the articles of faith as fundamental to a believer's behavior. This belief also extends to the inerrancy of the particular religion's scriptures and a duty to follow religious prescriptions, as these represent *truth*. Such fundamentalism is represented in all the world's faiths. Modern interpretations of these scriptures constitute a greater sensibleness in applying religious tenants in everyday life, even though the tendency towards secularism has diminished these foundations over time. As a result, individual believers that see their religion's practices diminished are motivated towards fundamentalism as a means to insulate themselves from such influences. What is perhaps the most misunderstood about fundamentalism is that the true believer strives to return to the founding principles of the religion rather than become a backward member of society, as perceived by the nonfundamentalist. What this means, in the practical perspective, is that true believers seek the simplicity of thought and emotional assuredness through the religion's belief structure, while still being able to function within modern societies. This is not always easily accomplished.

A major conflict between a society and religion's scripture occurs when the believer is viewed as backward (i.e., overly fundamental) despite their individual contributions to society. When enough believers come to see their society as inadequate to their underlying scriptures and practices, they tend to seek either seclusion, such as the Amish communities; the creation of a religious state, such as with many Middle Eastern and central Asian countries; or attempt to change the state's structure to adopt the religion's moral codes, such as with the Taliban-ruled Afghanistan. In democratic societies, these religious underlyings tend to be diffused by countervailing forces such as secularism and may result in political extremism, which may eventually lead to armed conflicts if a compromise cannot be reached. It is at this point that the actualization of the desired changes in the state and society by the religious fundamentalists resemble those of the contemporary political radical. According to Taylor and Horgan (2001), political radicals and religious extremists share the same processes in achieving their goals (i.e., destabilization and overthrow of the existing regime), and as such, are likely to establish working relationships with each other in order to share knowledge and intelligence, despite that they ultimately have different desires and outcomes. It should be noted that history has plenty of examples where philosophy diverges at some point in a political movement, resulting in excessive hardships for the citizens of toppled regimes.

The Islamic philosophy writings of Sayyid Qutb call for the empowerment of those seeking to make religion the only moral authority that extends to all aspects of life. This includes a nation's government, and can certainly be considered radical in modern times by Western countries and dictatorships alike. The same could be said of Karl Marx in the creation of communist-styled states, or the application of Charles Darwin's writings on the policies of the German society and the holocaust. The result of these writings being implemented by so-called revolutionaries created death tolls in the tens of millions throughout the world.

While terrorism has been conducted for many different reasons, the current focus of the world appears directed towards Islamic extremism, but the real issue runs so much deeper than simple labels. Is it possible that what is emerging as a radicalized version of Islamic philosophy is actually a new political movement that threatens the established methodologies of the West through the use of old forms of sustained conflict? Ideology and epistemology are perhaps the most dangerous forces in societal change, and it is this issue that creates the momentum of terrorism despite the enormous suffering it causes. History has and will continue to show that in the wake of destruction, it is ambitious, ruthless leaders of terrorist groups that seek to rebuild civilization in their own image, regardless of what claims are made to justify the suffering. The claim of a small group of people appealing to the larger group does not make it so, despite all the accepted rhetoric. It is in actions that the true orientation of intent becomes transparent.

The threat of terrorism has many forms, which operate at different levels of the social, national, and international orders. To understand the impact of terrorism, it is necessary to first gain an understanding of the different applications of terrorism in achieving armed and social change. In the following sections, an overview of terrorism at the domestic, international, and global perspectives will be presented.

Domestic

Domestic terrorism is essentially terrorism directed at the terrorist's own country on his or her own particular people. "Terrorism must have a purpose, one uses terror, violence, and intimidation to achieve an end. The system of government may use a system of terror to rule, and they would use fear and subjugation to achieve these aims. Those opposing a government may use terror to coerce public opinion to achieve their aims" (Tyler, 2002). Throughout world history and current times, there are examples of domestic terrorist groups seeking a change in governmental policies, separatist movements, and the call for an existing domestic government to be dissolved. There have also been governments that used terror to come into and/or remain in power. In Columbia, the Revolutionary Armed Forces of Colombia (FARC) and other narco-terrorist groups have repeatedly responded to crackdowns by the government's military with terrorist attacks against civilian targets. These have included car bombings (i.e., El Nogal Club and others), murders of antidrug support personnel, and the kidnappings of foreigners and Columbians. Ac-

Figure 2. Francisco Franco

cording to the U.S. Department of State, most indigenous terrorist and Muslim separatist groups that reside in Indonesia, Malaysia, Philippines, and Thailand are primarily focused on bringing about changes in their own respective country. In addition, over the past three decades, the Spanish government has continued to fight violent independence-minded Basques who are essentially armed radical leftists, as well as right-wing extremists that desire the return of the days of brutality that took place during the reign of Francisco Franco.

The use of intimidation, political strife, and economic consequences to achieve power and influence daily operations in the governing of a country falls into a terrorist's or government's use of terrorism in attaining domestic control. These will be discussed in the following sections.

Intimidation

Change can be a very scary thing for some people, and when change is forced upon groups not ready to accept it, domestic terrorism is one likely conse-quence. One way domestic terrorists seek to bring about change is through consistent intimidation of citizens and political officials alike. This intimidation usually comes in the form of violence against select targets that are either creating these unwanted changes, or against the beneficiaries of the changes. When the Civil War ended, white supremacists groups like the Ku Klux Klan began terrorizing African Americans with the burning of homes and the public hanging of individuals. These attacks were intended to "put the negro in his place," and demonstrate that no government is going to tell "good, law abiding citizens" how they are going to live. More recently in Bangladesh, a grenade attack was responsible for the deaths of 13 people as a result of an assassina-tion attempt by Hikmat al-Jihad (HAJ) on Sheikh Hasina, who narrowly survived the attack. Hasina is Bangladesh's second woman to ever hold the post of prime minister, and leader of the government's opposition party. Ivy Rahman, a women's activist, was among those killed. For some groups, terrorism sees women as agents of social change, and seeks to moderate or eliminate their capacity to institute change through violent intimidation. Free-dom of thought and self-expression is not the only action terrorists seek to control through intimidation.

Diversity, and the open movement of peoples within and between nations, are occurring more and more every day. This, in turn, leads to a greater understand-ing between nations and their citizens, at least for those that see a greater good from such exchanges. However, this also involves changes in how we moderate our prejudices and reconcile our pasts. As a result of Egypt's acceptance of an Israeli state in the Middle East, vacationing Israeli's regularly run the risk of being attacked by militants who seek to persuade the Egyptian government to sever ties with Israel. Other extremist groups in Egypt seek to dismantle Hosni Mubarak's government because it is viewed as secular, and as such, is considered illegitimate by a host of domestic terrorist groups. This fear of multinationalism and so-called secularism can be a major motivation for domestic terrorist efforts. During the occupation of the post-Saddam Iraq rebuilding efforts, Iraqi terrorists have kidnapped Americans, Britons, Egyptians, Indians, Italians, Japanese, Nepalese, Pakistanis, and a host of other perceived *invaders*, and have successfully intimidated some governments to withdraw from Iraq in order to isolate Iraq from the changes that these participants have been working towards. Successful intimidation often emboldens the insurgency, and is further supported by nationalistic pride in unity, regardless of the means employed. It should not be underestimated.

Political Strife

Violence is not the only means for terrorist organizations to enact domestic change. In many cases, terrorist groups have actively participated in the political process as an additional form of leverage to further their causes. The Basque Homeland and Liberty (ETA) movement in Spain, Hamas in Palestine, Kurdish extremists in Iraq and Turkey, the Irish Republican Army (IRA), the Muslim Brotherhood in multiple countries, the Tamil Tigers in Sri Lanka, and many more, from their beginnings, have had political wings in order to participate in and contest elections, as well as further so-called humanitarian efforts towards its own citizens. These efforts are complemented by the military wings of these organizations, which engage in armed combat, and have assigned high-value targets for assaults and assassinations. By having a division between the political and military operations, the political leadership can claim they had no knowledge of any given activity by the military branch, while being given greater acknowledgment regarding any future consequences when positive negotiations fail to occur.

As a natural extension on the discussion of political wings, another area of political strife resides in the democratic systems afforded most Western societies. Religious and ethic minorities in democratic countries have the "right" not to be assimilated by the collective, while actively participating in elections

Figure 3. Hitler's SA

to further political change. Where religious and ethnic ideologies meet, terrorists may utilize these intersections to have a larger, public political support base to draw upon, and therefore tend to have greater political longevity. Where public political support is not enough to further their respective causes, groups may invoke acts of terrorism and limited military actions to further their political ambitions. This tag team approach, where the political arm steps back and allows the military arm to act, and vice versa, creates long-term domestic upheavals with considerable consequence. This is especially effective in emerging or weak democracies such as post-World War I Germany.

There is an argument that shows that some terrorism can result in a given group's leader holding the top political post, such as president or prime minister. Adolph Hitler became Chancellor after first using the Sturm Abteilung (i.e., storm troopers, brown shirts, etc.) to do his dirty work to "clean up society" and remove any opposition that could threaten his political movement upwards. Once Hitler had a firm hold on all aspects of the government, he ruthlessly disbanded the SA leadership, and ultimately replaced it with the SS. This is but one example of a democracy being politically moved into a dictatorship through the use of terrorism.

Once ruthless terrorists get into power, brutality and social re-engineering becomes the norm. Stalin's gulags, Mao's re-education camps, the extermination camps of Hitler, and Pol Pot's killing fields of Cambodia are just some of history's more gruesome examples of radical political movements succeeding in obtaining power and then going horribly wrong.

Economic Consequences

Domestic terrorism does not just deter tourists from visiting a given country. It can effectively be used to inhibit business supplies and the natural flow of customers, make the cost of doing business in a region so high that it is commercially infeasible, and undermine confidence in an economy's underlying infrastructure. The result would be increased or excessive unemployment, social unrest, and monetary and market devaluations. Also, a given country's antiterrorism efforts add an inherent cost to supply and to maintain. Government coffers are filled at the expense of the population it services, and as a result, nothing provided is free. Such an environment is the breeding grounds for more recruits to help change the domestic policies of a country and seize power to enact change.

While reviewing the domestic terrorism literature, legislative hearings, and the like, the economic consequences are continually sited as a primary reason for fighting terrorism. What is not sighted is just how much domestic terrorism costs its citizens in specific economic terms. The cost to rebuild or repair a building or damaged street, or replace a destroyed vehicle can be quantified. The decrease of a country's gross domestic product can be calculated. The immigration, or the lack, of skilled people can be reported. The transfer of investments and savings to locations outside a country can be accounted. The problem lies in connecting a series of activities with terrorist acts, while discounting the effects of competitive forces, poor management of the business, legal and judicial environmental changes, and excesses by vested interests. It has been estimated that nearly 1.5 trillion dollars was lost in the aftermath of the September 11th attacks, but estimates are all we have. It is this author's belief that while no one can truly quantify the value of a life, the true economic consequences of domestic terrorism are either being ignored, being covered up, or are simply incalculable. This is an area that must be further researched and communicated to not only businesses, but the general populace, so an awareness of said consequences can be fully understood.

Global

The term globalization means enacting a process of interconnectivity and interdependence at a global or worldwide scale. Whether this is conducting trade, military force efforts, or establishing worldwide telecommunications, the term involves a multitude of nations and interested entities. As the U.S. is considered the primary driver of this process, the U.S. and its allies have become the focus of terrorist groups that seek to inhibit such a process. At the same time, such organizations seek to utilize the globalization process to expand their own influence, increase their access to resources, and maximize the effect of each and every attack. There are several primary influences driving the globalization of terrorism. These are media exposure, minority solidarity, the development of extremist subgroups, and the formation of subgroup confederations.

Media Empowerment

Martyrdom is yet another aspect to political change. It feeds discussions, reflections, and future ramifications to peace. It is supposed to show the ultimate resolve of a group to pay any cost for obtaining their goals. Unfortunately for those who have given their lives in a senseless act of taking someone

Figure 4. Hamas martyrs (www.nahost-politik.de/terror/kamikaze.htm)

else's life, it historically has only lead to the polarization and alienation of the sponsors of such acts when dealing with the existing governmental powers. The immediate consequences of so-relabeled homicide bombings and the like are protracted loathing of those who could encourage children, women, and men to blow themselves up, or commit an act that kills innocent victims, while extinguishing their own life. The notion that life is cheap and expendable actually counters the notion that modern societies should acknowledge and respect any group that encourages such acts.

Bombers willing to kill others along with themselves have occurred in many eras. The most notable of these were the Japanese kamikazes, who did little to change the war's outcome, though they did scare a lot of sailors. What appears to be gained through these types of acts is an understanding that someone determined to make a life and death statement is likely to be heard, but in most cases only once. The message dies with the individual along with their victims as a so-called last act of desperation.

The use of young Arabs or Asians blowing themselves up at checkpoints, bus stops, and restaurants, only to be rewarded at Heaven's gates, is nothing new. What is encouraging more of this type of attack is the high visibility it is being given to audiences that will likely never be involved in one. The media loves to broadcast and report on such incidents, and with the global information infrastructure, can do so on a moments notice. David Witzthum, the Chief Editor of *Israel Television*, stated that the "media is itself a weapon of the conflict—used by governments, rebels or terrorists alike, to achieve their goal —which is to show the effects of terror and violence. Their conviction is that the actual effect of terror is its representation in the media, without which its value and effect as weapon is meaningless and limited" (Witzthum, 2005). Displaying the gruesome has, without a doubt, created a new power in the arsenal of terrorists. The more sensational, the more terror is inflicted on people not exposed to such acts. In regions where such acts are readily occurring, travelers and business interests tend to pick other areas of interest to pursue as a result. The media must accept their contribution towards these ends. In not mitigating their responsibility, it also allows for a sense of solidarity to be developed around the world when such acts occur.

Minority Solidarity

Throughout the 1980s, internal conflicts and limited civil wars occurred in Algeria, Egypt, Syria, and Tunisia. The result was that the established regimes suppressed these conflicts, and many of the insurgent leaders fled to other countries within the region, and to any Western countries that accepted asylum. From these new locations, these leaders began establishing support structures among sympathetic ethnic and religious peoples, while enjoying the new protections of the new host country. Muslim Brotherhoods began to emerge, and they effectively utilized Web sites and ethnic newspapers to report from around the world any and all violence against Muslims, in order to incite, solicit, and exploit a cultivated sense of powerlessness within the Muslim community.

Another source in the creation of solidarity has been the use of satellite television, which allows preachers to promote cultural isolationism, civil disobedience, and solicit individuals to adopt a unification strategy for a particular faith or ethnicity. Listeners are encouraged to embrace the notion that, while an individual may posses the credentials of a given nationality, their true loyalty must be to their religious and ethnic roots. These broadcasts occur in safe Western havens, while reaching people in remote and isolated nations around the world.

Solidarity is not just an ethnic and religious phenomenon. Solidarity has cross-dimensional aspects that solicit a broad spectrum of interests and socioeconomic participants. Through the exploitation of a sense of solidarity by a cross-spectrum of minority groups within larger cosmopolitan communities, terrorists have been able to develop fund-raising schemes, acquire educated and skilled recruits, obtain logistical and intelligence support, and even apply significant pressures for the political suppression of reactive governmental responses and multilateral participations. Such solidarity cannot be underestimated as a powerful mechanism to the fulfillment of an extremist group's agenda.

Extremist Subgroups

When it is considered that the world's population is approximately 6 billion people, even a small percentage of countercultural people can number in the tens of thousands on a global basis. Radicals, anarchists, religious fundamentalists, and insurgency groups are everywhere and in every form. These groups come into existence when conditions within a country allow like-minded individuals to share their discomfort while identifying with other like-minded groups for inspiration. With the advent of the World Wide Web, ideologically oriented extremist groups can display their doctrines, perspectives, and agendas. It is the acquisition and acceptance of these groups' ideas that cause so many of them to appear indistinguishable from each other, and facilitate the spontaneous creation of new groups as current events unfold. In 1995, four Saudi Arabians admitted to being inspired by Muslim militant groups when they attacked and blew up a U.S. military facility in Riyadh, which resulted in the deaths of seven people, even though they stated they had no direct association.

How individuals come to participate in these types of groups is derived from a concept that emphasizes the personal as the political. By participating in some form, the individual learns to operationalize a group's ethics. Within a group of people, ethical rules emerge from the collective. Groups tend to have weak powers of discipline, and strong powers of integration and inclusion. Group solidarity is usually displayed and actualized in initiatory rituals and stages of membership, and marked by espousing the shared values and ideals of the collectivity. By joining a group, an individual seeks to have a function in society, and as such, plays a role in society through the group. It has been shown that groups tend to operate more morally than its individual members, which is a scary thought considering what extremists groups have done in the past, and what they are capable of doing in the future. Through basic societal processes, extremist groups are able to solicit weak-minded people that feel a need to *belong* and *contribute* as well as the recruitment of strong-willed individuals that seek to influence the direction of society. These groups exist as subcultures within and without their own societies. As these groups extend their reach outwards, affiliations and confederations will continue to emerge.

Subgroup Confederation

There is little doubt that the global information infrastructure has facilitated the sharing of ideas, knowledge, and coordination of terrorist organizations, and this will be presented in greater detail in later chapters. It has, in essence, permitted the creation of a network of terror networks, and provides the infrastructure for global criminal syndicates as well. The lines between politically motivated terrorism and criminal syndicates are ever increasingly being blurred by similar processes. Where groups share vested interests in terrorist outcomes, collaborations tend to occur on a global basis. Where groups do not share outcomes, territorial issues come into play. Criminal organizations generally do not want to see a society thrown into chaos, as it disrupts business as usual, and may very well facilitate the downfall of terrorist organizations operating in their self-proclaimed jurisdictions. Therefore, the creation of confederations takes time, and requires the building of trust between groups,

Figure 5. Red Army Faction symbol

and may well be a point of exploitation that can be used by governments seeking to disrupt such collaborative networks. Where common-interest groups do collaborate, improvements in the acquisition and sharing of intelligence information, training and skills acquisition, and material supply support can occur. An example of this is Italy's Red Brigade, Japan's Red Army, and West Germany's Red Army Faction, all of which collaborated with the Palestinian Liberation Organization in the use of training camps and coordinated attacks, such as the seizure of the OPEC Summit meeting held in Vienna in 1975. These groups also continued to pursue their own agendas within their respective countries while maintaining joint operations. It is therefore critical for governments to work towards breaking down these collaborations.

With the fall of the Soviet Union, as previously discussed, a void was created in the coordination and support of terrorist groups on a global scale. Groups such as al Qaeda have chosen to fill this void by specializing in bringing disparate groups around the globe together by providing funds, training, and structural logistics. It is groups like al Qaeda that are particularly dangerous to modern societies, as they can incite a relatively small, powerless group of people to emerge as a well-organized, coordinated, and skilled terrorist group by facilitating the flow of resources from state sponsors. Additionally, by encouraging the participation in various jihads around the globe by these small groups, new skills are transferred, a renewed sense of trust and purpose between groups is established, and added incentives and rewards are granted to terrorist groups and their respective leaders for their so-called successes. In this author's opinion, this area is one of the most important aspects that must be addressed in securing our world today.

Final Thoughts of This Chapter

Fear of violence is a very real issue, and must be addressed by all participants at all levels of a society. Power, the quest for more power, or more importantly, the lack of power will create dysfunctions throughout a given society, and in a globally connected world cause the spread of these dysfunctions as they will be reported by interested parties. It is a natural law that when a power exists, a lesser countervailing power is automatically created. Thus, there will always be opposition to the status quo, and in some cases, this opposition will be violent. How we, as a society, choose to resolve this opposition says volumes about ourselves, and perhaps the likelihood of our future as a society. The true test of democracies lies in integrating subcultures into the mainstream, while maintaining the unique contributions of such groups. This must be embraced universally at all societal levels of a nation, or segregation, and its resulting fear and hatred, is likely to occur. We, as a society, must be able to determine what must be embraced and what must be discarded in as moral a method as humanly possible. Otherwise, we may create a new generation of terrorists, and diminish the will of society to eliminate terrorism.

The domestic, international, and global aspects of terrorism have a host of divergent beginnings, and as such, have no one approach to pacifying any given terrorist's activities. In all cases, terrorist groups that take innocent life have no regard for the concept of self-determination, except when considering their own desires. Anyone who believes in and supports such groups has a basic societal dysfunction that is longitudinal (i.e., skewed) to modern democratic societies. In this author's opinion, these dysfunctions are breeding widespread support for an ever-evolving form of extremism, resulting in the widespread proliferation of violent acts. As a result, the threat of terrorism is evolving faster than modern societies seem to be able to compensate. So serious is this problem, that at the G8 Summit held in France in 2003, an action group of donor countries was established to provide any willing country seeking to combat terrorism, with the supporting resources to enact financial, immigration, customs, arms trafficking, and law enforcement programs, including efforts towards cyber surveillance and cyber security efforts.

From this point on, the role that information technology plays in facilitating terrorist goals, agendas, and activities shall be presented. In the following chapters, the focus of this book will be on the use of the global information infrastructure and in particular the use of cyberspace by terrorists.

References

Conference of Foreign Ministers, Kuala Lumpur, Malaysia, April 1-3, 2002. (2005). *Kuala Lumpur declaration on international terrorism*. Retrieved from http://www.oic-oci.org/english/fm/11_extraordinary/declaration.htm

Energy Information Administration (EIA). (2005). *International gross domestic product, population, and general conversion factors information*. Retrieved from http://www.eia.doe.gov/emeu/international/other.html#IntlGDP

Flemming, P., & Stohl, M. (2000, September). Myths and realities of cyberterrorism. *International Conference on Countering Terrorism Through Enhanced Cooperation*. Retrieved from http://www.comm.ucsb.edu/Research/Myths%20and%20Realities%20of%20Cyberterrorism.pdf

Taylor, M., & Horgan, J. (2001). The psychological and behavioural bases of Islamic fundamentalism. *Terrorism and Political Violence, 13*(14).

Tyrer, H. (2002). Cyber-terrorism. *Science and technology of terrorism and counterterrorism*. New York: Marcel Dekker, Inc.

U.S. Code of Federal Regulations Title 22, Section 2656f(d).

Witzthum, D. (2005). The Israeli-Palestinian conflict: The role of the media. *Media, conflict and terrorism — Speeches and issues notes*. Retrieved from http://mandela.inwent.org/ef/media/witzthum.htm

World Islamic Front. (1998, February 23). *Jihad against Jews and Crusaders*. Retrieved from http://www.fas.org/irp/world/para/docs/980223-fatwa.htm

Additional Readings

Beck, U., & Beck-Gernsheim, E. (2002). *Individualization, institutionalized individualism and its social and political consequences*. London: Sage Publications.

Boyle, G. (2002). Theories of justification and political violence: Examples from four groups. *Terrorism and Political Violence, 14*(2).

Breinholt, J. (2003, July). Philosophy of American terrorism crimes. *Terrorist Financing, 51*(4).

Burdman, D. (2003). Education, indoctrination, and incitement: Palestinian children on their way to martyrdom. *Terrorism and Political Violence, 15*(1).

Capgemini & Merrill Lynch. (2004, June). *World wealth report.*

Committee of Privy Counsellors. (2004, July). *Review of intelligence on weapons of mass destruction.* United Kingdom House of Lords.

Cragin, K., & Daly, S. (2004). The dynamic terrorist threat, An assessment of group motivations and capabilities in a changing world. *Project Air Force.*

Crelinsten, R. (2002). Analysing terrorism and counterterrorism: A communications model. *Terrorism and Political Violence, 14*(2).

Donohue, L. (2001). In the name of national security: US counterterrorist measures, 1960-2000. *Terrorism and Political Violence, 13*(3).

Durham, M. (2003, June). The American far right and 9/11. *Terrorism and Political Violence, 15*(2).

Emerson, S. (1997, August 4). The terrorist infrastructure. *Wall Street Journal.*

Gerecht, R. (2002, April 8). They live to die. *Wall Street Journal.*

Gordon, A. (2001). Terrorism and the scholarly communication system. *Terrorism and Political Violence, 13*(4).

Gulati, R., & Gargiulo, M. (1999, March). Where do interorganizational networks come from? *The American Journal of Sociology, 105*, 177-231.

Hiebert, M., & Brauchli, M. (2004, September 23). India sets focus on better life in rural regions; Singh believes his nation may show path to coping with Islamic aspirations. *Wall Street Journal.*

Higgins, A., Chazan, G., & White, G. (2004, September 16). Battlefield conversion: How Russia's Chechen quagmire became front for radical Islam; Aligning with Arab militants gained money, fighters for rebel leader Basayev; Swapping 'Che' for Allah. *Wall Street Journal.*

Hobman, E., Bordia, P., & Gallois, C. (2003). Consequences of feeling dissimilar from others in a work team. *Journal of Business and Psychology, 17*(3).

Hookway, J. (2002, October 21). Terrorist bombings hit Philippines — Series of weekend explosions kill 10 people, highlighting militants' threat to region. *Wall Street Journal.*

Hufbauer, G., Schott, J., & Oegg, B. (2005).*Using sanctions to fight terrorism* (Policy Brief 01-11). Retrieved from http://www.iie.com/publications/pb/pb01-11.htm

Israeli, R. (2002). A manual of Islamic fundamentalist terrorism. *Terrorism and Political Violence, 14*(4).

Israeli, R. (2002). Western democracies and Islamic fundamentalist violence. *Terrorism and Political Violence, 12*(4).

Joint Chiefs of Staff. (2002, October). Antiterrorism personal protection guide: A self-help guide to antiterrorism. *CJCS Guide 5260.*

Kabbani, S. (2003). *The approach of Armageddon? An Islamic perspective.* Islamic Supreme Council of America.

Khan, M. (1999, September). Shura and democracy. *Muslim Democrat, 1*(2).

Knapp, M. (2003). *The concept and practice of jihad in Islam.* Parameters.

Maffesoli, M. (1996). *The time of the tribes, the decline of individualism in mass society.* Sage Publications.

Melloan, G. (2004, October 12). Why the election will change Afghanistan. *Wall Street Journal.*

National Commission on Terrorism. (2005). *Countering the changing threat of international terrorism.* Retrieved from http://www.gpo.gov/nct/

National Commission on Terrorist Attacks Upon the United States. (2003, May). *Hearing of the National Commission on Terrorist Attacks Upon the United States, Day 2, Civil aviation security.*

National Commission on Terrorist Attacks Upon the United States. (2003, October). *Hearing of the National Commission on Terrorist Attacks Upon the United States, Fourth public hearing, Intelligence and the War on Terrorism.*

National Commission on Terrorist Attacks Upon the United States. (2004, July). *The 9/11 Commission report.*

Nedoroscik, J. (2002). Extremist groups in Egypt. *Terrorism and Political Violence, 14*(2).

Nichols, M., & Day, V. (1982, March). A comparison of moral reasoning of group and individuals on the "Defining Is…". *Academy of Management Journal, 25*(1).

Perl, R. (2005). *Terrorism, the media, and the government: Perspectives, trends, and options for policymakers* (CRS Issue Brief). Retrieved from http://www.fas.org/irp/crs/crs-terror.htm

Post, J., Sprinzak, E., & Denny, L. (2003). The terrorist in their own words: Interviews with 35 incarcerated Middle Eastern terrorists. *Terrorism and Political Violence, 15*(1).

Sedgwick, M. (2004). Al-Qaeda and the nature of religious terrorism. *Terrorism and Political Violence, 16*(4).

Surowiecki, J. (2004). *The wisdom of crowds, why the many are smarter than the few and how collective wisdom shapes business, economies, societies, and nations*. New York: Doubleday.

Testas, A. (2001). The economic causes of Algeria's political violence. *Terrorism and Political Violence, 13*(3).

Trimble, D. (2004, September 2). The lesson of Northern Ireland. *Wall Street Journal*.

Tucker, D. (2001, March). Combating international terrorism. In J. M. Smith, & W. C. Thomas (Eds.), *The terrorism threat and U.S. government response: Operational and organizational factors*. USAF Institute for National Security Studies.

United States Department of Justice, Federal Bureau of Investigation. (2004, April). *Report to the National Commission on Terrorist Attacks Upon the United States: The FBI's counterterrorism program since September 2001*.

United States Department of the Treasury. (2001, September). *Terrorism, what you need to know about U.S. sanctions*. Office of Foreign Assets Control.

United States House of Representatives. (2004, December 7). *Intelligence Reform and Terrorism Prevention Act of 2004*.

Weinberg, L., Pedahzur, A., & Hirsch-Hoefler, S. (2004). The challenges of conceptualizing terrorism. *Terrorism and Political Violence, 16*(4).

Wentz, L. (2002, July). Lessons from Kosovo: The KFOR experience. *CCRP*.

Chapter III

Cyber Terrorism Evolution

Objectives of This Chapter

√ Begin to discern the connection between terrorism and technology.

√ Understand the evolution from hackers to crackers, crackers to cyber criminals, and cyber criminals to cyber terrorists.

√ Identify the key elements that comprise the term cyber terrorism.

√ Become familiar with the support role that a cyber terrorist can bring to a terrorist organization.

√ Understand the potential collaborations between criminal organizations and terrorist groups in attaining cyber skills.

Introduction

Coined by William Gibson in his 1984 book *Neuromancer*, cyberspace is referred to as the virtual realm of electronic communications allowing community interaction, and information storage and retrieval. Cyberspace continues to evolve, and so does its exploitation by all interested parties. A subset of cyberspace is a particular classification of science fiction known as cyberpunk. Cyberpunk deals with the exploration of the impact that cyber technology has on society. Today's cyberspace is no longer science fiction, but instead has become an integral aspect of modern societies, and extends beyond conventional theorizing. Cyberspace is here, now, and must elicit consideration beyond fantasy, hype-oriented media channels, and naive so-called intellectuals. One noteworthy component of cyberspace is the Internet.

In an examination of the supporting infrastructure impacted by the World Trade Towers attack, in *Information, technology, and coordination: Lessons from the World Trade Center response*, it was stated:

> *From the beginning, the Internet worked when other networks failed, providing telephone and text messaging service to key City officials, supporting emergency management applications, and keeping citizens informed of progress.* (Dawes, Birkland, Tayi, & Schneider, 2004)

This is quite remarkable, considering the enormity of damage inflicted by the subsequent collapse of the buildings, and the state of organization of the public and private sectors in the vicinity. This communication channel allowed a reduction in panic while resources were brought to bear. For without it, the panic and fear derived from these attacks well could have been far greater. Now remember, terrorism is about inflicting fear through violence. Eliminating a supporting infrastructure, even for a short period of time in a physical crisis, reveals an inherent weakness in our dependence on that infrastructure, and furthers the goal of creating fear and panic. The supporting nature of cyberspace makes it a potential target as a force multiplier when combined with another, future physical attack.

In a statement reported to Hamid Mir of the Ausaf newspaper, Osama bin Laden said, after the September 11th attacks that "hundreds of young men had pledged to him that they were ready to die and that thousands of Muslim scientists were with him and who use their knowledge in chemistry, biology and ranging from computers to electronics against the infidels." Since this statement was printed, it has been reported that:

- Encrypted, detailed plans for destroying airliners were on Ramzi Yousef's laptop computer.
- Osama bin Laden's aides utilized encrypted e-mail to transmit the September 11th attack instructions to Mohammed Atta.
- Supervisory control and data acquisition (SCADA) system Web sites have been accessed by al Qaeda members in order to gather intelligence on these potential targets. (SCADA systems are used to monitor and control utility equipment such as power and water distribution systems).
- Al Qaeda-owned computers were found to have structural and engineering data associated with dams.
- Khalid Ibrahim, a member of the Pakistani terrorist group Harkat-Ul-Ansar, is known to use social engineering methods to gain information on hacking into U.S. military networks.
- Al Qaeda prisoners, during interrogations, have stated their intentions to use computer network tools to further their goals.

These are the clear beginnings of terrorist organizations becoming aware of the use and exploitation of information technology. It would appear that there is definitely a degree of technological skill to terrorist operations, and they must not be underestimated. Also, terrorist organizations have shown that they are capable of not only utilizing technology, but of turning it against us (i.e., turning jetliners into missiles). In this chapter, an examination of the basic evolution of a cyber terrorist shall be presented. This evolution begins with a very brief history of the computing industry and the emergence of networking. This, in turn, will introduce the concepts of hackers and hacktivism, crackers and cracking, and then an introduction to cyber crime. From this foundation, a cyber terrorist role in support of terrorism will be offered.

Bits and Chips

From the times of the Colossus project at Blechley Park in England, and the development of the electronic numerical integrator and computer (ENIAC), computers have utilized vacuum tubes and electro-mechanical controls, and filled up large rooms. These machines were not only the first great leap forward in computing; they operated in isolation and secrecy in the early 1940s. In the 1950s, computers such as the Universal Automatic Computer (UNIVAC), began making their way into the business community as business machines performing data processing. With the incorporation of transistor and integrated circuit technologies, computers began appearing in large business and government facilities as mainframes in the 1960s. Integrated circuit developments allowed computers to become smaller and faster, while the invention of the modulator-demodulator (MODEM) allowed digital computers to communicate via standard analog telephone lines. It was the development of the first dynamic random access memory (RAM) chip and the first microprocessor that began a new era in computing in the 1970s with the creation of minicomputers and microcomputers. When these were coupled with the newly created Advanced Research Projects Agency network (ARPAnet), the Internet began its early evolution towards its current incarnation. Services such as messaging, e-mail, Telnet (i.e., a protocol service for controlling computers remotely), and file transfer protocol (FTP) for transmitting files between systems, were now available to a limited number of people covering a large geographic area. These developments continued to increase throughout the 1980s and 1990s, resulting in more powerful processing capabilities, smaller physical sizes, expanded telecommunication connectivity, and a more robust network with the establishment of the National Science Foundation network (NSFnet) infrastructure. New protocols and standards were established for the network of networks as millions started surfing the World Wide Web in the 1990s.

Over the past decade, whole new innovations in digital technologies have propelled the usage of networks into every aspect of business and government operations. These operations have their own particular agendas including profit, societal governance and control, and ultimately, possession and power over information in this so-called Information Age. These new technologies have changed the way societies digest information, and as a result, affect how new knowledge is formulated. Essentially, knowledge is an understanding of the information acquired from the learning experience, and if this experience is shaped, predicted outcomes can be the result.

Because society has, and continues to struggle with the methods and consequences of controlling information, self-interested parties continue to assert their perspectives on the development and use of cyberspace by various means. Controlling this new medium allows one to control the flow of information, and therefore gain some additional measure of power over society. As previously discussed, a power that exists automatically creates a lesser, countervailing power, and cyberspace with all its stakeholders is no different. This central realization creates a host of countervailing and exploitative entities such as hackers, crackers, cyber criminals, and most importantly to this text, cyber terrorists.

Hacking and Hactivism

For over 20 years, this author has witnessed every possible politically motivated definition of just what constitutes the term *hacker*. In the early days of computing, hackers were considered more in terms of being a technology geek, rather than some evil computing force that destroys systems. The term hacker encompasses programmers that enjoy exploring the limits of computer technologies. This includes everything from games, business applications, landline and satellite communication systems, and networks of every kind.

Traditionally, hackers saw themselves as innovators and activists for the improvement of the industry, and sought the elevation of their prowess amongst self-reported peers. They examined software and systems for bugs and weaknesses, most often without the permission of the owners, and at their own expense. They developed solutions for free distribution known as freeware and shareware. Hackers readily published their results amongst academic journals and nonacademic venues alike (though some now institutionally established hackers would disagree with this perspective). In many cases, they reported their findings directly to the business interest in question in hopes that improvements would occur, and continue these activities today.

At the core of many within the hacker community, it is thought that all software should be free or at least relatively inexpensive after it was developed, creating the notion of open source software. Any individual or organization that seeks continued returns from their software were/are considered greedy by the hacker community. When software companies began making enormous profits from the computer industry as a result of the coding foundations of many unpaid hackers, a fundamental split in the hacker community on the whole occurred. Persons of nonutopian perspective began to emerge as disruptive, destructive, and exploitative towards these profiteering business and governmental interests. Through their activities, these *hackers* brought about punitive consequences upon the hacker community as a whole. It became necessary for businesses to promote the development of new laws, and the enforcement of existing laws, to prevent unauthorized entry and theft of proprietary information, as well as to prevent the interruption of on-going business efforts and services. In an effort to distance themselves from these persons, the hacker community created the term *cracker*, and this term will be discussed in the next section of the chapter.

While there are still many in society that insist on combining the term hacking with cracking, what truly separates these two groups is legal activism. Throughout the Internet, one can find countless manuals on legal hacking, showing just where the legal lines reside, and these manuals make it abundantly clear not to cross them. The reason for this legal line is founded in the basics of data communications. The very nature of communications requires an initial *handshaking* between the two connecting systems. Fundamentally, this is the equivalent of two people initiating a conversation by first asking in what language they will be speaking, and what rules will be adhered to during the conversation (i.e., protocol). This means that the initialization phase between two systems is an open dialog, and subject to observation (i.e., modern eavesdropping). Other systems, such as Web sites, have stored files in the open, as these are required for requested services and functions of connecting and/or serviced systems (i.e., Web services lookup tables, etc.). These too are subject to a hacker exploring their structure and contents. In order to use the services available through an Internet service provider, a user must be granted certain access rights within a system. The use of these rights to view resources, itself constitutes *legal* hacking, as access was granted as a subscriber of the service. Where hacking crosses the line into cracking is when files are modified or copied without implied permissions. This author advocates checking with a lawyer before believing anyone as to what is the current version of legal hacking, as this line changes as a result of judicial rulings and prosecutor activism seeking to expand on existing law through the courts.

What lies behind a hacker's motivation for exploring the capabilities of a system is founded in personally challenging his or her skills, as well as a rationalized element of activism. Hactivism (i.e., hacking combined with activism) is the use of computing resources in a legal manner to solicit societal change. One very interesting and well-established development in the realm of hactivism is the use of cyber sit-ins to forward social activism. A form of electronic civil disobedience, these sit-ins solicit large numbers of Internet users (i.e., sometimes up to 10,000 people) to visit a given Web site or Web facility at a given time, simultaneously. This effectively causes a quasi-legal distributed denial of service attack on the targeted facility. Because there are so many user requests of the targeted facility occurring at the same time, service is disrupted and/or prevented to anyone else attempting access. In many cases, the organizers distribute software to participants that target specific services to be made unavailable during these joint visits. Generally, participants in cyber sit-ins come together to protest some activity in the physical world such as a war, legislative proposals, and other societal and political agendas.

This domain (i.e., hacking) continues to shrink in scope as computer software licensure agreements, copyright laws, and national security legislation continue to restrict the use of software and communication systems for nonspecified purposes. Licensure agreements state that the software is owned by a given company, and as such, the user must agree to the terms and conditions before permission is granted to use it. What this means is that the agreement to restrictions, such as the decompiling of the software's source code, may be deemed a breach of the agreement, and potentially a violation of civil and/or criminal laws. Also, legislation such as the Digital Millennium Copyright Act of 1998 makes it a crime to:

- Bypass antipiracy mechanisms built into commercial software.
- Manufacture, sell, or distribute software-copying devices that crack copy protection mechanisms.

The act also makes an Internet host system responsible for licensing fees of content distribution by its members (i.e., music downloader sites like Napster), and requires them to remove copyrighted content from their users' Web sites. There are, however, some exemptions to the cracking of protection devices as a matter of research in product interoperability and penetration testing, but these are severely restrictive, and are still being carefully reviewed by the hacking community for legality as ongoing court cases establish precedence. Ultimately, the hacking community will continue to explore areas that have no established legal consequences, while leaving illegal activities to the crackers.

Crackers and Cracking

Building upon the basic skills acquired as a hacker, crackers have and continue to explore the "opening up" of computer systems for their particular desires. Crackers enjoy the challenge of breaking into forbidden structures to acquire whatever prize is waiting as a result of their skill. The desire to break an encryption algorithm, disable a game's antitheft mechanism, or even create tools that provide an unfair advantage over other participants in an online game are but a few examples of cracker activities. Regardless of the legal aspects of cracking, these individuals carry forward many of the social rationalizations of hackers to justify their exploitation of incomplete, weak, and/or commercialized systems.

One area that crackers excel in is destructive testing. This term is used literally, in that crackers break protective mechanisms and bring down weak systems. Destructive testing has a social value in that attention by interested parties is usually given to weaker systems only when they are disrupted or broken. The evolution of the software security industry has been in response to ever increasingly sophisticated attacks against computer and networked structures. While this is by no means a rationale for illegal behavior, crackers tend to view destructive testing more as a public service than a criminal act.

Another carry over from the hacking domain is a discontent of profiteering and anticommercialization. The notion that companies should reap the lion's share of profit from the work of others troubles people in all societies. Crackers actively decompile software to decipher the inner workings of protection mechanisms, document these mechanisms for future cracking efforts, and release the cracked version of the software to the whole of the Internet and traditional sales venues. Throughout much of Asia, cracked versions of software such as Microsoft's Office, popular games, and many others are available for pennies on the dollar in storefronts. This is one area that crackers cross the line and enter the ranks of cyber criminals for the widespread distribution of cracked products, and will be discussed in the next section of this chapter.

The most distinguishing aspect of crackers that impacts the whole of the computing industry is the development and global distribution of exploit engines. An exploit is a piece of software that exploits a known vulnerability in another software package, which can then be used to hijack or disable the package in order to enact some other end result. Imagine that a company employs a firewall hardware/software solution at their Internet connection point. Now, a firewall's function is to hide the internal network's Internet protocol (IP) address from the outside world, control the flow of data packets through various ports (i.e., logical data communication channels) in both incoming and outgoing directions, and control program access through these ports. Even if this firewall was properly configured and installed, it may still have an unknown weakness within its core programming. A hacker or a cracker may discover this vulnerability and notify interested parties as to how to penetrate the firewall. What may happen is that an exploit may get created, specifically designed for this firewall, which requires very little skill in deployment (i.e., script kiddies) and may be used to bring down and/or penetrate the firewall. Additionally, this exploit may allow its user to customize the desired outcome once the firewall has been accessed. Because exploits are usually widely distributed and made readily available to anyone wishing to use it, this particular firewall brand and its subsequent customers are in real trouble. The net result is that the firewall's manufacturer has a reliability problem, a commercial liability issue that must be resolved promptly, and a public relations nightmare requiring fast mobilization to prevent competitors from taking their market share, while millions of Internet junkies download and use the exploit to access and disrupt networks. The manufacturer will effectively need to create a fix quickly to eliminate the vulnerability that may require a firmware or software update. Such a scenario is happening on a daily basis throughout the world.

The production of software is far from flawless. In many cases, vulnerabilities are published by the manufacturer before a widespread attack has occurred in order to announce that a software patch is available to correct the problem. These announcements are intended for system administrators to access the new patch or update, and install it on their respective systems. When these patches are not installed, exploits that have been created for a given patched vulnerability can be used to create havoc throughout systems connected to the Internet and/or other connected systems (i.e., private networks such as banking ATMs). The Code Red worm virus is a classic example of using a known buffer overflow weakness in systems that had not been patched by system administrators. As a result, over 250,000 server hosts were penetrated and temporarily disabled. This easily could have been far worse if the Chinese programmers had decided to do more than simply order the hijacked servers to launch a distributed denial of service attack against the U.S. White House's Web site. The computer skill level needed to use most vulnerability exploits is relatively low, while the skill to develop one can be quite high.

Cracking computer systems requires various skill sets in hardware, software, and networking environments. These foundational skills can initially be learned through university-level course work, scores of self-help books, and a lot of personal practice time. Once a cracker achieves a high level of expertise in breaking and breaking into systems, what then are these skills used to accomplish? It is this author's opinion that a major divergence occurs within the cracker community at this point. One group continues on illegally challenging systems for personal glory and social activism, while a smaller group turns to the exploitation of their skills through being employed by or creating criminal organizations.

Cyber Criminals and Cyber Crime

Wherever there are robust societies, opportunists will emerge with less than honorable intentions. Crime is nothing new, and the world of cyberspace will continue to have its fair share. A crime is considered to be an unlawful act, and if found guilty of committing one, results in some form of punishment. Computer crime is considered by most governments to be committing an unlawful act with a computer. Cyber crime is not so clear, and is often considered computer crime by default. Cyber crime may consist of the acts discussed in the preceding cracking section, the selling or transport of contraband in cyberspace, the theft of property including people's identities, and a host of other offenses deemed inappropriate by societies and governments alike. This is a pretty large net that is cast to catch criminals that use cyberspace to commit crime. In reality, the larger the impact on societal and business interests, the more resources that will be brought to bear on cyber crime.

Throughout the 1980s, there were some very notable, high-profile cases that caused businesses and governments to institute new laws and enforcement policies. These included:

- Three West German spies penetrating the computer system at the Lawrence Berkley Laboratory. These spies acquired confidential electronic documents on the Strategic Defense Initiative (i.e., Star Wars), and semiconductor designs. The thieves were apprehended after astronomer Cliff Stoll noticed the computer intrusions and conducted his own investigation, resulting in the arrests of the spies and the publication of the story entitled *The Cuckoo's Egg*.

- The first so-called hacker celebrity, Kevin Mitnick, emerged after a series of stunning accomplishments resulting in his subsequent arrest and conviction. These exploits included the theft of intellectual property, and the free use of long distance telephone service, as well as the reported deletion of his criminal record from police and court system records.

In more recent history (1998), thieves using cyber stealth techniques penetrated U.S. military computer networks over a number of years, which resulted in the downloading of a large number of "sensitive technical files." The so-labeled Moonlight Maze investigation by federal authorities tracked the thieves as far as Moscow, and they have not been apprehended to date. In 2003, Romanian cyber criminals penetrated the National Science Foundation's South Pole Research Station, and enacted a blackmail scheme that consisted of a demand to be paid off or the station's data would be given to other countries. Once the threat was validated, Station officials had to temporarily shut down the penetrated system. This was the same system that controlled the Station's environmental controls in a -70° Fahrenheit harsh environment.

In a 2002 report by the Center for Strategic and International Studies, James Lewis states:

> *Emphasizing the transnational nature of cyber security issues, the last few years have seen the emergence of highly sophisticated criminal gangs capable of exploiting vulnerabilities in business networks. The aim is not terror, but fraud or the collection of economically valuable information. Theft of proprietary information remains the source of the most serious losses.*

What this means is that cyber criminals have become well organized, highly skilled, and have been targeting specific assets to sell. It also means that in order to reduce or eliminate such activities, a multilateral approach involving countries from around the world is required as criminal organizations that exploit computer network technologies tend to ignore national borders.

Because cyberspace encompasses multinational jurisdictions, cyber criminals circumvent prosecution by operating in countries that have either weak or nonexistent computer crime laws, or lack the resources for strong enforcement of such laws. The ease in which a computer crime can be committed is in stark contrast to the lengthy process of acquiring permissions to accessing transaction and tracking information from all systems participating in the chain of events, as well as deducing what actually transpired and from where. As a result, governments from around the world have established cooperative treaties and conventions to facilitate the enforcement of cyber law in an attempt to discourage and prevent cyber crime. These agreements are designed to promote the creation of consistent computer crime law, provide for cooperative investigations, encourage the enforcement of these laws, and provide for extradition when these laws are broken. As a result, jurisdictional issues are diminishing as these efforts move forward.

The G8, which consists of Canada, France, Germany, Italy, Japan, Russia, the United Kingdom, and the United States, established the High-Tech Crime Subgroup in 1997. The group's purpose was to develop comprehensive, substantive, and procedural computer crime law so that no safe haven would exist for such perpetrators. In 2001, the Council of Europe Convention, and in 2002, the Commission of the European Communities established computer crime articles in an effort designed to control the growing threat of cyber crime. In addition, ongoing efforts continue to reduce this threat through the Organization of American States and the Asia Pacific Economic Cooperation to implement laws and enforcement procedures consistent with the rest of the world. However, finding out that a cyber crime has happened and actually doing anything about it is no simple process.

The process of catching cyber criminals can be lengthy, complex, and requires time and patience. Setting the cross-jurisdictional and transnational issues of cyber investigations aside, there are effectively three standard methods to catching cyber criminals. The first of these methods involves the use of audit and transaction logs which all networked computer system components maintain to back step the electronic path of the cyber criminal in hopes of obtaining their origination point(s). Law enforcement would then proceed with physical aspects of investigation involving interviews, telephone traps and traces, ongoing surveillance, and the confiscation and application of computer forensics in order to establish a case history to prosecute. The second method involves the creation of an attractive target known as a honey pot. People tend to follow the path of least resistance while being attracted to interesting or valuable items. Honey pots allow system administrators and law enforcement to provide an easily accessible target to potential cyber criminals, while hopefully having stronger security measures in other parts of their systems. When an intruder enters a honey pot (i.e., a computer server trap designed to entrap an intruder), transaction monitors and alarms detect the intrusion and track all activities of the intruder. This is generally the initial phase of tracing the individual to their point of origin, as well as of providing a greater understanding as to the intruder's intentions. From this point on, traditional electronic and physical investigation techniques can be employed to locate the individual(s) involved in the intrusion and/or theft. The last method is to utilize electronic monitoring devices such as the Carnivore system. What systems like Carnivore do is to intercept all Internet communications that flow through the monitored system. This includes Web browsing, file transfers, issued protocol commands, and e-mails. When these "boxes" are attached to an Internet service provider's server, the monitored user's Internet activities can be recorded for further analysis and/or prosecution. In most cases, judicial authorization is required and specific user accounts are identified for surveillance, but not in all cases. These three methods are essentially what cyber cops have to work with in the electronic frontier, excluding socially engaged entrapment techniques.

Law enforcement and governmental legislatures ultimately determine the labeling of criminals and the application of law on a given individual's actions. Where this delineation occurs is dependent on current events and society's particular focus. As with the migration of hackers moving into the community of crackers, cyber criminals with suitable incentives and motivations can be encouraged to move into the cyber terrorist arena. So where do we draw this line between cyber crime and cyber terrorism? Are we actually interested in focusing our current efforts on identifying and punishing terrorists? Such a delineation must not be a matter of external factors by simply relabeling or reclassifying an individual's actions. In this author's opinion, becoming a cyber terrorist requires the adaptation of a terrorist group's goals, and as such, must become a new classification operating on a different paradigm of cyber crime, and this will be discussed in the next section of this chapter.

Cyber Terrorism and Cyber Terrorists

Throughout academia, business, and governmental arenas, multiple perspectives on the hype or validity of the notion of cyber terrorism have been considered and published in conferences, journals, white papers, and commissions alike. The differences in perspective have their origins in defining exactly what should encompass the activities of cyber terrorism. These definitions have included everything from the convergence of cyberspace and terrorism to "severe economic damage" (Denning, 2001). The truth of the matter is that because no such legislatively defined meaning exists, the domain is open to debate, dispute, and ultimately, ambiguity.

Similar to any industry, new concepts are applied to previously discussed areas in an attempt to further define and develop the concept. Some are accepted while others are wholly rejected. In a 1998 report by the Center for Strategic and International Studies entitled *Cybercrime, Cyberterrorism, Cyberwarfare, Averting an Electronic Waterloo*, one of the first commonly accepted definitions for cyber terrorism was put forward. Cyber terrorism can be defined as:

> *Cyberterrorism means premeditated, politically motivated attacks by subnational groups or clandestine agents, or individuals against information and computer systems, computer programs, and data that result in violence against noncombatant targets.* (Center for Strategic and International Studies, 1998)

In 2004, before the Senate Judiciary Subcommittee on Terrorism, Technology, and Homeland Security, the Deputy Assistant Director of the Cyber-Division of the FBI Keith Lourdeau defined cyber terrorism as:

> *a criminal act perpetrated by the use of computers and telecommunications capabilities, resulting in violence, destruction and/or disruption of services, where the intended purpose is to create fear by causing confusion and uncertainty within a given population, with the goal of influencing a government or population to conform to a particular political, social or ideological agenda.* (Lourdeau, 2005)

The main problem with these two definitions is that both view an individual as a cyber terrorist. This means that if an individual does not like what a government is doing, and in response decides to communicate this disagreement by changing a government department's Web page in a manner that elicits fear in someone viewing it (i.e., fear is being considered violence), that individual is now a cyber terrorist as a result of their political inclination and illegal computer actions. There are many historical accounts of people trying to make a nonviolent political assertion (i.e., by legal or illegal means) that causes people in society to shudder in fear. Modern societies must clearly distinguish between the fear that may be caused by an individual's political orientation or assertion, and any physical violence enacted. Otherwise, societies may never evolve or overcome outdated ideologies, and spend enormous effort on symptoms instead of root causes.

The whole antiterrorism movement is predicated on the notion that there are organizations actively working to injure and kill innocent people throughout the world. In this author's opinion, a clear linkage between these organizations and an individual's computer criminal activities must be established before labeling anyone a cyber terrorist. As simplistic as this may sound, before we as citizens, businesses, and governmental organizations can take focused, directed action against cyber terrorism, we must first clearly identify just what our target is going to be. This author proposes a compromise definition of the previous definitions as follows:

> *Cyber terrorism is a premeditated, politically motivated criminal act by subnational groups or clandestine agents, against information and computer systems, computer programs, and data, that results in physical violence, where the intended purpose is to create fear in noncombatant targets.*

Working from this definition, accidental hackers, individual crackers, and financially minded cyber criminal individuals and organizations would not be considered cyber terrorists. Also, attacks against combatant targets would fall outside this definition, and instead would be considered cyber warfare. Such a definitional scope for cyber terrorism does not, however, alleviate any criminality under current laws, nor excludes computer crime as serious, but such criminal acts must be tied to physical terrorism. Simply put, new cyber terrorism law must distinguish between past computer criminal acts by incorporating physical violence as an outcome perpetrated by terrorist organizations. Once this is resolved, initiatives towards eliminating it can begin to be developed, and if possible, help secure systems from all categories of computer crime.

To further this point, Deputy Assistant Director Keith Lourdeau stated: "As our nation's economy becomes more dependent on computers, and the Internet becomes an increasingly more integral part of our society, new digital vulnerabilities make U.S. networked systems potential targets to an increasing number of individuals including terrorists" (Lourdeau, 2005). What this means is that by working to secure cyberspace in general, additional mechanisms will be put in place to prevent terrorists from attacking this infrastructure. But before anyone can defend against a cyber terrorist attack, one must examine the potential targets, attack methods, and the overall usage of the infrastructure by terrorists. The last of these, in part, is what will be discussed in this section, while the remaining items will be brought forward in future chapters.

Communication, Coordination and Information Sharing

The global information infrastructure provides the ability for terrorists with great distances between them to communicate via voice (i.e., landlines, satellite, and voice over Internet protocol), file transfers, electronic mail, and chat sessions. Groups may also use Web site postings for activity dissemination and recruitment. Because terrorist groups can now operate in a distributed, networked structure, communication technologies have become a critical asset to these organizations. Within individual terrorist groups or cells, members can operate over greater geographic regions, performing independent tasks while having the capability of maintaining frequent communications that are required in the support of terrorist tasks and operations. Because any given terrorist organization binds its members to its long-term goals (i.e., state collapse, injuring a so-called great evil, etc.), a group can maintain its identity without a shared location through the use of communication technologies. In addition, informational access to similar groups, methods, and technical knowledge can be accessed via public networks to supplement an individual or group's capabilities or insights.

When alliances between groups have been created, more specific logistical and technical information, and shared knowledge can be accessed directly between cell leaders. This shared access may be segmented and/or restricted by individuals higher in the command structure for security and control purposes. Segmentation minimizes the likelihood of the entire structure being compromised either through intelligence gathering or betrayal. At this distributed cell coordination level, cell leaders can share resources, intelligence, and coordinate objectives, as well as communicate directives between each other. It should be noted that over time, these collaborative relationships will either be strengthened by the value of shared assets, or diminish when divergent interests or limited assistance capabilities occur.

The control over terrorist groups and/or cells is maintained by transmitting orders from the respective leadership down the chain of command, while all members transmit information and intelligence upwards to important individuals in the structure. This essentially creates a dynamic, robust system that provides the foundation for coordination efforts and feed back from its members' activities (see Figure 6).

Through an effective communication and control structure, terrorist groups can coordinate individual member efforts, facilitate resources that allow for the basic maintenance of the group, and make available specialized skill sets to allied groups. The skills required for utilizing this basic communication structure are not very advanced if circumventing surveillance techniques is not required. Even with the additional use of encryption to hide the content of various communications, these types of individuals would be considered cyber assisted terrorists, and can easily be trained by conventional education methods. The moment that eavesdropping, audit trails, trace routes, and other origination

Figure 6. Command and communication structure

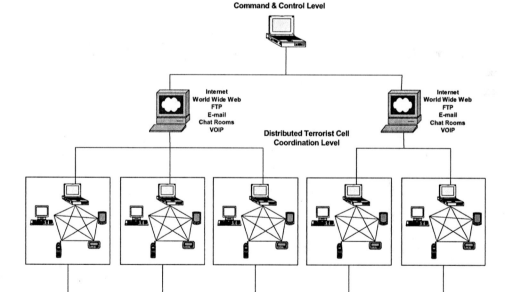

detection tools are employed by government agencies, specialized skills in computer science and network technologies become required to hide critical aspects of terrorist communications and electronic transactions. These cyber terrorist skills will be presented throughout the rest of the book as the global information infrastructure and cyber attack scenarios are offered.

Activity Dissemination

Without a public audience, terrorism is limited and rendered impotent to all who are not directly affected. As part of a terrorist group's ongoing activities, the brazen display of its criminal acts are facilitated through the use of Web sites, newsgroups, and the like. These postings may be controlled by terrorists, or by those who are willing to post such information for "public" consumption (i.e., sympathizers and exploiters). According to the AntiTerrorism Coalition's (ATC) Database of Terrorist Web sites and e-Groups at http:// www.atcoalition.net/, there are over 1,000 Web sites, e-groups, and forums that support the promotion and dissemination of terrorist activities. The ATC was one of the first public organizations to track and document these activities. As a result of their systematic identification of these sites, the ATC has provided a valuable tool for businesses and governments to systematically shut down these sites for abuses in user agreements and violation of law.

Some Web sites seem to be the first to offer the public the most gruesome of terrorist organizations' acts. The display of the beheadings and executions of Ala al-Maliki, Barea Nafea Dawoud Ibrahim, Eugene Armstrong, Jack Hensley, Ken Bigley, Fadhel Ibrahim, Firas Imeil, Khaled Abdul Messih, Kim Sun-il, Luqman Hussein, Murat Yuce, Nick Berg, Paul Johnson, Robert Jacob, Georgi Lazov, and many others have been initially posted as a means of creating

Figure 7. Video threats and beheadings

terror in those viewing them. In fact, many a news channel has downloaded such videos and used them in national broadcasts. The basis for uploading such videos is quite simple once you have acquired the video footage. Either the initial footage was recorded on a digital camera, and this file was directly uploaded, or the video is run through a conversion process that digitizes the content. This in turn is uploaded to the Web site and made available for all to see.

Throughout much of the second Iraq war, several of these beheadings were uploaded to Web sites hosted in Malaysia, which are reported to have links to al Qaeda. These uploads have records associated with their transactions, and as such, the source location of the upload can be determined. With the proliferation of cyber cafes and free wireless networks, such tracking has its limitations and further investigation requires additional intelligence. It should also be noted that the owners and the operators of such Web sites have some serious explaining to do before government investigators providing jurisdictional restrictions have been eliminated. Unfortunately, the nature of the Web allows for transnational maintenance of Web site content. Therefore, all that can effectively be done is for such sites to be shut down, and their operators be investigated, which is what happened with the Malaysian sites.

Cyber Terrorist Tasks

Cyber terrorists exist today. The Osama bin Laden Crew (OLB Crew) is a group of self-proclaimed cyber jihadists. This group is reported to have been founded in 2000 by Abdullah Quraischi, an al Qaeda member living in Europe. The group's activities have consisted of the creation of dozens of Web sites and forums that provide information on gun making, explosives manuals, as well as large-scale recruitment promotions and propaganda (AntiTerrorism Coalition, 2005). Remember, the overarching concept about cyber terrorism emerges where terrorism meets cyberspace. As previously stated, this takes the form of facilitating the underlying communications and control infrastructure of terrorist organizations, and also includes the dissemination of a group's activities, as well as the facilitation of knowledge exchange. But this is only the beginning in understanding what a cyber terrorist does (i.e., reported and unreported), and may yet still do.

In general, a cyber terrorist will use the global information infrastructure to gather intelligence on potential targets by accessing both public and private systems by whatever means necessary (i.e., external break-ins, insider assistance, as an employee, etc.). Once a high-value target has been established, a cyber terrorist may facilitate or enhance the effect of a physical attack. For instance, the disabling of emergency medical service (EMS) communications prior to blowing up a commercial building would be considered a force multiplier in instilling public fear and furthering any resulting injuries. With more and more of our lives falling dependent on computerized, networked systems, a cyber terrorist also has the ability to attack high-value targets remotely. Imagine that a city official is having open-heart surgery. This official's blood type is stored in a medical database. What would happen if this blood type was remotely changed and this change went unnoticed? This is but another example.

Much of the focus being expressed by concerned interests about potential attacks by cyber terrorists is in regards to SCADA systems. SCADA systems are used to monitor and control utility equipment such as power and water distribution systems. The loss of statewide power grids, the contamination or disruption of water distribution, or the deliberate opening of a dam's flood waters are but additional targets that have been penetrated in the past, and may in the future be employed by cyber terrorists to cause harm. The fact that there have been a multitude of proposals to electronically connect these systems on a national scale only creates the potential for additional widespread havoc. These and other critical infrastructures will be further expanded upon in future chapters.

Final Thoughts of This Chapter

In this chapter, the evolution of the cyber terrorist and how they may be of use to a terrorist organization was examined. Additional skills and capabilities will be brought forward in future chapters. But how a person gets to this level of skill and beyond is but one half of the issue. Why someone would work so hard to get to this point only to be destructive is the other half. In this author's opinion, the nature of progressive societies is to challenge the status quo. The culture of hackers and crackers has evolved from this notion. From their cultural foundations lie many of the skills required to move into criminal and terrorist activities in the cyber world. Competing for financial gain is one thing, but trying to destroy one of the sources of power that can be used to bring about change is another. Or is it that the global information infrastructure is just a vehicle that will be metaphorically packed with explosives and driven to its destruction taking as many lives with it as possible?

There are two primary differences between criminals and terrorists in cyberspace: the transfer of knowledge about these systems, and the destruction of the system. No self-respecting criminal would gladly share their acquired knowledge in order to create a potential rival. This cannot be said to be the same for a cyber terrorist. Because of their ideologies, the sharing and transfer of skills and abilities is not only encouraged, but may very well be a fundamental requirement in furthering their respective *causes*. No self-respecting cyber criminal would hand the keys of a vehicle to a cyber terrorist knowing that their source of income is about to be taken on a one-way ride. It is this author's hope that the vested self-interest of hackers, crackers, and cyber criminals to maintain their continued contributions and/or exploitations of cyberspace will not allow their skills to be easily transferred to terrorists. However, once these skills are transferred (i.e., perhaps through purchase or deception), they will be documented and proliferated quickly to terrorist groups throughout the world. This needed awareness is one of the main motivations for writing this book.

References

AntiTerrorism Coalition (ATC). (2005). *Database of terrorist Web sites and e-groups*. Retrieved from http://www.atcoalition.net/

Center for Strategic and International Studies. (1998). *Cybercrime, cyberterrorism, cyberwarfare, averting an electronic Waterloo*.

Commission of the European Communities. (2005). *Creating a safer information society by improving the security of information infrastructures and combating computer-related crime*. Retrieved from http://europa.eu.int/ISPO/eif/InternetPoliciesSite/Crime/CrimeCommEN.html

Council of Europe. (2001, November). *Convention on cyber-crime, explanatory report*. Retrieved from http://conventions.coe.int/Treaty/en/Treaties/Html/185.htm

Dawes, S., Birkland, T., Tayi, G., & Schneider, C. (2004, June). *Information, technology, and coordination: Lessons from the World Trade Center response*. Center for Technology in Government.

Denning, D. (2001, December). Activism, hacktivism, and cyber-terrorism: The Internet as a tool for influencing foreign policy. *Internet and International Systems: Information Technology and American Foreign Policy Decisionmaking Workshop.*

Gibson, W. (1984). *Neuromancer.* New York: Berkley Publishing Group.

Jihad Watch. (2005). Retrieved from http://www.jihadwatch.org

Library of Congress. (1998). *Digital Millennium Copyright Act of 1998.* Retrieved from http://thomas.loc.gov/cgi-bin/query/z?c105:H.R.2281.ENR

Lourdeau, K. (2005). *Testimony of Keith Lourdeau, Deputy Assistant Director, Cyber-Division, FBI, before the Senate Judiciary Subcommittee on Terrorism, Technology, and Homeland Security. Cyberterrorism.* Retrieved from http://www.fbi.gov/congress/congress04/lourdeau022404.htm

Stoll, C. (1989). *The cuckoo's egg.* New York: Pocket Books.

Additional Readings

Anonymous. (2002, August). Cyber-security: Key to homeland security. *Information Management Journal, 36*(4).

Blitzer, R. (2005). *Domestic intelligence challenges in the twenty-first century.* Retrieved from http://www.lexingtoninstitute.org/homeland/Blitzer.pdf

Bosch, O. (2002, May). Cyber-terrorism and private sector efforts for information infrastructure protection. *Creating Trust in Critical Networks Workshop of the ITU Strategy and Policy Unit.*

Bostom, A. (2004, May). The sacred Muslim practice of beheading. *FrontPageMagazine.com.*

CERT Coordination Center. (2005). *International coordination for cyber-crime and terrorism in the twenty-first century.* Retrieved from http://www.cert.org/reports/stanford_whitepaper-V6.pdf

Dearne, K. (2002). Cyber-crime boom. *Information Management & Computer Security, 10*(5).

Denning, D. (2000, May). *Cyber-terrorism, Testimony before the Special Oversight Panel on Terrorism Committee on Armed Services, U.S. House of Representatives.*

Denning, D. (2001). Activism, hacktivism, and cyber-terrorism: The Internet as a tool for influencing foreign policy. *Networks and netwars: The future of terror, crime, and militancy.* Retrieved from http://www.rand.org/publications/MR/MR1382/

Denning, D. (2001). Cyberwarriors: Activists and terrorists turn to cyberspace. *Harvard International Review, 23*(2).

Embar-Seddon, A. (2002). Cyber-terrorism. *The American Behavioral Scientist, 45*(6).

Engelman, A., Goldstein, H., Lange, D., & Peterman, C. (2000). International Chamber of Commerce creates cyber-crime unit. *Journal of Property Rights, 12*(2).

Flemming, P., & Stohl, M. (2000, September). Myths and realities of cyber-terrorism. *International Conference on Countering Terrorism Through Enhanced Cooperation.* Retrieved from http://www.comm.ucsb.edu/Research/Myths%20and%20Realities%20of%20Cyberterrorism.pdf

Groves, S. (2003). The unlikely heroes of cyber-security. *Information Management Journal, 37*(3).

Holland, C. (2005). *The Carnivore Internet monitoring device: Capabilities, statutory framework, and constitutional considerations.* Retrieved from http://www.as.uky.edu/polisci/courses/PS%20491 Carnivore%20Paper-Canon.pdf

Iyengar, J. (2004). A discussion of current and potential issues relating information security for Internet communications. *Competitiveness Review, 14.*

Jachowicz, L. (2003, January). *How to prevent and fight international and domestic cyber-terrorism and cyber-hooliganism.* Retrieved from http://honey.7thguard.net/essays/cyberterrorism-policy.pdf

Janczewski, L. J., & Colarik, A. M. (2005). *Managerial guide for handling cyber-terrorism and information warfare* (pp. 213-221). Hershey, PA: Idea Group Publishing.

Khanvilkar, S., & Khokhar, A. (2004, October). Virtual private networks: An overview with performance evaluation. *IEEE Communications Magazine.*

Lawson, S. (2005). Information warfare: An analysis of the threat of cyber-terrorism towards the US critical infrastructure. *SANS GSEC.*

Lazarevic, A., Srivastava, J., & Kumar, V. (2005). *Cyber-threat analysis — A key enabling technology for the objective force (A case study in network intrusion detection)*. Retrieved from http://www.cs.umn.edu/research/minds/papers/asc2002.pdf

Milone, M. (2003, March). Hacktivism: Securing the national infrastructure. *Computer and Internet Lawyer, 20*(3).

Nagpal, R. (2002, September). Cyber-terrorism in the context of globalization. *Proceedings of the 2nd World Congress on Informatics and Law.*

Nisbet, C. (2004, January). Cyber-crime and cyber-terrorism. *Securing Electronic Business Processes — Highlights of the Information Security Solutions Conference 2003*. Vieweg.

O'Neil, M. (2001). Cyber-crime dilemma. *The Brookings Review, 19*(1).

Patterson, A. (2003, April). Fighting hackers, fraud, and wrong perceptions. *ABA Banking Journal, 95*(4).

Pollitt, M. (2005). *Cyber-terrorism — Fact or fancy?* Retrieved from http://www.cs.georgetown.edu/~denning/infosec/pollitt.html

Porcelli, N., Selby, S., Bagner, J., & Sonu, C. (2002, May). Bush administration endorses increased sentences for cyber-crimes. *Intellectual Property & Technology Law Journal, 14*(5).

Raghavan, T. (2003). In fear of cyber-terrorism: An analysis of the Congressional response. *Journal of Law, Technology & Policy, 1.*

Rogerson, S. (2003, August). Cyber-terrorism and the threat to democracy. *IMIS Journal, 13*(4).

Rubin, S., Smith, M., & Trajkovic, L. (2003, October). A Blackboard architecture for countering terrorism. *Proceedings of the 2003 IEEE International Conference on Systems, Man and Cybernetics.*

Sofaer, A., & Goodman, S. (2000, August). *A proposal for an international convention on cyber-crime and terrorism*. Retrieved from http://www.ciaonet.org/wps/soa02/

Stambaugh, H., Beaupre, D., Icove, D., Cassaday, W., & Williams, W. (2000, August). State and local law enforcement needs to combat electronic crime. In *National Institute of Justice Research in Brief*. National Institute of Justice.

Sterling, B. (1992, November). *The hacker crackdown: Law and disorder on the electronic frontier*. New York: Bantam Books.

Swartz, N. (2003). Are you ready for the next cyber-attack? *Information Management Journal, 37*(5).

Swartz, N. (2003). Controversial surveillance system renamed. *Information Management Journal, 37*(4).

Swartz, N. (2003). Cyber-crime code could punish online protesters. *Information Management Journal, 37*(3).

Tan, K. (2003). *Confronting cyber-terrorism with cyber-deception*. Master's thesis, Naval Postgraduate School.

United States House of Representatives Committee on Science. (2005). *Hearing charter: Cyber-terrorism — A view from the Gilmore Commission*. Retrieved from http://www.house.gov/science/full/oct17/full_charter_101701.htm

Verton, D. (2003). *Black ice: The invisible threat of cyber-terrorism*. McGraw-Hill.

Wagg, M., & Dinh, K. (1991, June). Satellite services for Australia in the 1990s. *Proceedings of the IEEE International Conference on Communications*.

Warren, M., & Furnell, S. (2005). *Cyber-terrorism—Political evolution of the computer hacker*. Retrieved from http://www.cyberguard.info/resource_center/WhitePapers/Cyber%20Terror.pdf

Weiler, N. (2001, December). Secure anonymous group infrastructure for common and future Internet applications. *Proceedings of the 17ᵗʰ Annual Computer Security Applications Conference*.

Chapter IV

Global Information Infrastructure

Objectives of This Chapter

√   Identify the major components of the global information infrastructure.

√   Begin to understand how communication network technologies are bringing the world closer together.

√   Come to understand the growing dependence that societies and businesses have on this infrastructure.

√   Discover the services, major mechanisms, and protocols that are used to secure the global information infrastructure.

√   Realize that the task of securing the global information infrastructure is an evolutionary process.

Introduction

Networks come in many forms. A network is essentially the connecting of two or more entities with the ability to communicate. Utilizing a multitude of telecommunication technologies such as the public switched telephone network (PSTN), public switched data network (PSDN), cable television (CATV) network, and orbiting satellite networks (i.e., commercial and military), people from around the globe can communicate and share information virtually in an instant. The real-time services that this infrastructure provides include regular telephone calls, video conferencing, voice over Internet protocol (VOIP), and a host of other analog, digital, and multimedia communications. Connecting these networked systems and facilitating their communications are high-speed switches, routers, gateways, and data communication servers. Combined, these technologies and infrastructures comprise the global information infrastructure (GII), which is primarily used for the sharing of information and data.

This infrastructure serves communications between communities; business, industrial, and distribution interests; medical and emergency services; military access; as well as air and sea traffic control systems. It also facilitates the coordination of peoples' activities and shared knowledge. As a result, the systems and subsystems that comprise the global information infrastructure are more often being designed and upgraded to create an interconnected, heterogeneous (i.e., consisting of dissimilar components), and distributed network of networks, which are becoming interdependent on each other (see Figure 8). While the economics of this unification may seem to be the primary motivation, it is where people's interests are concerned that there tends to be an economic focus.

In this author's opinion, the only rational understanding for this increased interconnectivity is that such a network of networks has incredible value in unifying peoples of different national, cultural, and ethic origins for their particular own self-interests. It serves as the foundation for a whole new level of communication between people and their specific interests. This has not gone unnoticed by terrorist organizations.

For terrorist organizations that are founded in an isolationist or minority radicalism orientation, the global information infrastructure presents an increased challenge to their ability to hold on to control of their respective territories, as well as the hearts and minds of the people they wish to preside over. They will continue to encounter more unity between nations and govern-

Figure 8. Simplified global information infrastructure

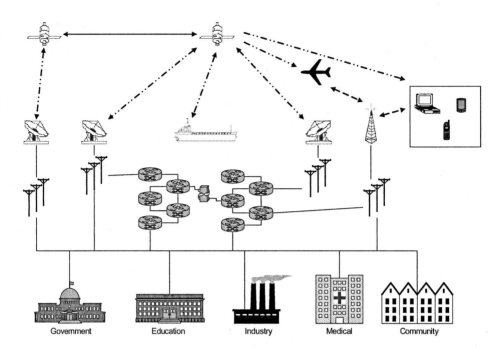

| Government | Education | Industry | Medical | Community |

ments as our respective cultures share knowledge and ideas. The net effect will be that terrorists will increasingly become marginalized by the vast majority of people if their ideologies do not have a shared, cultural value with the people they purport to serve while such a unifying global system exists. Therefore, radicals of all sorts will seek to bring harm to such a shared resource when it does not work to their advantage.

In order to better understand the capabilities that a cyber terrorist has and the potential impact on our day-to-day lives, an overview of the major telecommunication technologies employed within the global information infrastructure must be briefly presented. These include the role that telephone systems, satellites, and the Internet (i.e., circuit switching, packet switching, and mobile networks), and so forth, have in communications and will be presented throughout this chapter.

Telephone System

Alexander Graham Bell created the Bell Telephone Company in 1877. Since this beginning, talking to people has never been the same. As the telephone infrastructure evolved and incorporated computer technologies to facilitate the placement and routing of calls, so too did its standardization evolve, and eventually come to a consensus among telecom providers. What emerged was an architectural standard known as the Signaling System 7 (SS7) communication protocol. SS7 is used to support all calls made within a system, and between multiple public switched network systems. The protocol provides call addressing, call routing, and call handling based on a series of quality of service parameters such as traffic loads and security requirements. This standardization brings with it a common base for telecommunication systems to communicate, but it also provides the consistency needed to begin exploring any weaknesses within such systems.

As previously presented, telecom carrier intrusions are nothing new. Composed of circuit and packet switched networks, an intruder may by a variety of means obtain the original source code for a carrier's operation support systems (OSS) in order to develop a means to exploit the OSS. In exploiting a potential weakness in the OSS, a telecommunications system can be penetrated, and access to connected components and information can then be used to reconfigure the OSS and/or monitor transactions going through it. This provides an intruder with the capacity to reroute a call that is intended to go to a legitimate entity to one designated by the intruder and/or provide a means for remote eavesdropping of communications over landlines or mobile and data channels. In the practical sense, this means that a call that is placed to a known entity, such as local law enforcement, may in fact be routed to a criminal seeking to prevent the authorities from responding to a call for help. The person at this new receiving location may then present the appearance of being a policeman, take the call and all the details from the caller, put the caller at ease by telling them help is on the way, and then politely hang up. While such a scenario is unlikely in secured, highly developed telecommunication systems, the same can not be said of lesser-developed countries, or telecom providers that take security lightly.

Landlines

Ever since Cyrus Field laid the first transatlantic telegraph wire, transnational communications have enjoyed extensive usage. With more than a billion reported landlines in existence today, and nearly half of these having been installed in the last 10 years, more people and systems than ever before are communicating. Telecom carriers have offered wired "landlines" to businesses and residents alike for some time. Traditionally, multiple phones required multiple lines. As wire technology improved, it became possible to use different parts of the wire's transmission frequency to provide multiple services on the same wire, such as having regular telephone service combined with a digital subscriber line (DSL) for high-speed data transfers. With the advent of services such as call waiting and forwarding, caller identification, group calling, video conferencing, and data transmissions through the packet switch data network and integrated services digital network (ISDN) for digital services such as videotext, telex, telecommunication credit cards, and the like, these physical lines are needed and relied upon more everyday.

Data Transfers

Computers store and process digital data and information. Part of this processing is the communication and electronic transfer of data. For practical purposes, a data communication system transports data between users, user devices, and data terminal equipment. When data transmissions occur over analog lines (i.e., telephone lines), an initial conversion from its digital format into analog is done via a modulator-demodulator (modem). This, in turn, is used to impress data on an analog carrier wave that is altered to carry the digital data stream. Because transmission lines are being used in a manner that maximizes their capacity, multiplexers (MUX) are being used to share these communications lines for multiple uses. MUXs accept lower speed voice and data, and combine them into one high-speed stream for transmission. Because of these technologies, traditional voice communication systems are being displaced by all digital systems as increased demand for dual data transmissions on the same line continues.

A critical technology in digital telephone networks is packet switching. Messages and/or data streams that are to be sent through a packet switching system are subdivided into small packets for transmission. While there are a multitude of transmission mediums, the most common are fiber optic, coaxial cable, and twisted pair. The medium determines the general speed capacity, but it is the controlling protocols that determine how packets are subdivided, and the manner and order in which they are transmitted and forwarded. When transfers occur through asynchronous transfer mode (ATM) networks, messages are broken into small protocol data units (PDU) for packet switching. When these PDUs are forwarded, a virtual circuit path is created, and the packets are sequentially transmitted. The other dominant packet transmission used is a combined protocol approach known as transport control protocol/Internet protocol (TCP/IP). With this approach, messages are divided into small packets, but the forwarding path and order is left up to the routing system's metrics for quality of service. What this means is that packets from the same message may be routed through different paths.

The reason that an understanding of the underlying packet methods is needed is to understand the potential threats to interception and eavesdropping. If the data transfer of all packets occurs on the same path, and in sequential order, then a third party may record the entire transfer for later analysis by sitting anywhere on the transfer path. If different paths are used, then eavesdropping becomes more difficult, and requires that the eavesdropper view the data packets at the point of reassembly. Additionally, this understanding does not incorporate any protective mechanisms used to secure the unauthorized reading and/or modification of the packets, and will be discussed later in this chapter.

Mobile

Mobile users (i.e., citizens, police, EMS, military, etc.) place telephone calls, and transfer data (i.e., text messaging, e-mail, etc.) to landline and mobile users alike through a mobile-enabled device. Each mobile device (i.e., phone, personal digital assistant, laptop computer, etc.) is equipped with its own receiver/transmitter at a particular broadcast frequency. Radio waves that are analog are used as a carrier wave for such transmissions. Through a network of mobile towers and wireless access points that establish transmission connections via the radio wave frequencies, conversations and data transfers can occur without the benefit of being physically plugged into a telecommunication system. These towers and access points are physically connected to a given telecommunication carrier's network, and as such, may in turn provide access to the entire global information infrastructure.

Because mobile technologies rely on broadcast frequencies, information transmitted through the air is subject to monitoring. Devices such as pagers tend to receive broadcast data in clear text, while more sophisticated phone systems utilize spread spectrum and frequency hopping to limit surveillance. Spread spectrum is a wireless transmission approach that deliberately varies the transmission frequency between connected devices in order to encompass a larger bandwidth of surveillance. Frequency hopping makes use of the wider frequency range in that deliberate "hops" between frequency transmissions occur in order to minimize the unauthorized interception and/or jamming of a single frequency (i.e., frequency hopping code division multiple access [FH-CDMA]). As with all communications over unsecured channels, eavesdropping can occur unless additional security measures are implemented. The wireless medium is particularly prone to eavesdropping even when security mechanisms such as encryption are used. This is because the encrypted transmission is still broadcasted between the connecting devices and, given the ability to decipher such a transmission, the eavesdropper would then have access to the communication. Encryption and other security mechanisms will be presented later in this chapter.

Cable

Cable television is a transport system for television and radio content through coaxial cabling. According to the Directorate for Science, Technology, and Industry Committee for Information, Computer, and Communications Policy in a report in 2003, there are over 163 million cable television subscribers (OECD, 2003). Cable subscribers are increasingly including broadband Internet subscriptions with their television access, as this medium provides speeds that far exceed DSL and ISDN capabilities. Subscribers are also adding telephone service through this medium (i.e., voice over Internet protocol). VOIP enables people to make telephone calls by sending voice transmissions via packets through the Internet to another Internet user, traditional or cellular telephone user. While these additional services are a minority of the total subscription, they continue to grow rapidly each year.

Cable networks can be considered hybrid structures in that their core infrastructure is fiber optic cabling combined with coaxial cabling that connects homes and business units to core hubs. Cable networks can be said to plug into other telecommunication systems in order to provide additional services beyond radio and television broadcasts (i.e., Internet, VOIP, etc.). Depending on the availability of regional content providers, satellites are utilized to transmit and receive content as well. These services and their content are then distributed throughout the cable network. In the next section, satellites will be presented.

Satellites

There are thousands of satellites in orbit around the earth. Satellites can best be viewed as an electronic retransmission device that receives electromagnetic signals and retransmits them over a wide geographic area (i.e., satellite foot print). Satellites may also have the capability for intrasatellite communication between each other via radio frequency and point-to-point laser transmissions. Satellites tend to take up a geostationary orbit in order to provide a consistent service area. The principle services that satellites provide are the cross-continental and global retransmission of data in all forms, location and navigation information, as well as surveillance and espionage data. These include the following:

- Provide one- and two-way broadcasts between senders and receivers, such as satellite television and telephone services.

- Make available global positioning systems (GPS) that are used by transport ships, airplanes, trucks, and everyday drivers alike.

- Relay emergency radio beacons via satellites for rapid-response teams to locate downed transports.

- Disseminate news media content through simultaneous distribution to multiple sites (i.e., all recipients within the satellite's foot print).

- By combining the use of a powerful camera lens, satellites can view troop movements, the construction of facilities, and even the logo of a person's baseball cap.

Whether the use of surveillance satellites is being viewed in real time or through the use of historical images over a period of time, events and activities can be

Figure 9. Satellite image of Cairo provided by SpaceImaging.com

documented and used for strategic planning, tactical responses, and account-ability for past transactions and/or deeds. Such information is not always restricted, and/or may be intercepted by those unauthorized to do so.

The data that is transferred through satellite systems has varying value depen-dent on the particular needs of the interceptor. A commonly understood aspect of satellite broadcasts is that the transmissions simply need to be unscrambled for analysis of the critical data and information being transmitted. This is possible because of the broadcast aspect of the technology, and has lead to many successful attempts in order to simply get free television service.

For those seeking to steal, usurp, or bypass (i.e., not be observed) such services, the first step is identifying the location and capabilities of a given satellite. There are many public and private sources to identify and locate satellites (see Figure 10). The information contained by these sources show a satellite's longitude and latitude, its uplink and downlink frequency ranges, its beacon telemetry, and its operational status, among other items. This type of

Figure 10. ORBVIEW 3 satellite data (http://www.fourmilab.ch)

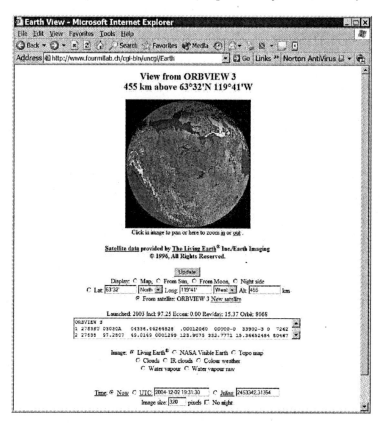

information allows for a host of interactions with the unmanned satellite, many of which are not necessarily intended. The jamming of the broadcasts and/or the remote hijacking of a satellite's controls could be used to disrupt or replace throughput transmissions. While this may seem like science fiction or fantasy, it has been reported that the Chinese-outlawed spiritual group Falun Gong has on several occasions hijacked a Chinese satellite by breaking its security codes and uplinked content to the satellite in order to broadcast its own perspectives to serviced users in mainland China.

In more remote regions of the world, or when mobility is required, many satellite service providers now offer connectivity services such as Internet access, which in turn make available all the various communication vehicles provided by the Internet. In the next section, the Internet's basic services and core protocols will be briefly presented.

Internet

The Internet is a global collection of interconnected networks. According to the International Telecommunication Union (ITU), there are over 145 million Internet hosts servicing over 600 million users worldwide. The Internet is continuously being integrated into, and facilitated by, the previous technologies discussed in this chapter. As a result, its infrastructure has a major impact on the global information infrastructure.

The primary protocol that governs the Internet's communications between computers and components is TCP/IP. Using this and other protocols, there are many services that use the Internet infrastructure to provide the dissemination and facilitation of information and data flows. These are as follows:

- The main user interface into the Internet is the World Wide Web. It is a collection of Web servers that support specially formatted documents that can be viewed using a Web browser. With over 8 trillion Web pages (Google.com, 2005) in existence, these documents support links to other documents, graphics, and audio and video files, using a language known as Hypertext Markup Language (HTML). It should be noted that not all Internet servers are Web enabled.

- The main vehicle for the transfer or posting of content files is file transfer protocol (FTP). In the same way as HTML transfers Web pages, this protocol allows files to be exchanged between servers and/or end-user systems. This protocol is most often executed as a subfunction of another program.

- One of the oldest terminal emulation programs still in use today is Telnet. This program allows a user to enter commands remotely as if they were at the server console. In this way, an administrator or intruder can remotely control an Internet server through a Telnet session.

- Electronic mail (e-mail) is the Internet's most ubiquitous application. The underlying protocol that governs e-mail is simple mail transfer protocol (SMTP), which is a protocol for sending e-mail messages between mail servers. The retrieval of these messages then occurs by using the post office protocol (POP) or Internet message access protocol (IMAP) to download them from the server to a mail client (i.e., an e-mail application program). File attachments to these messages often occur as well, and are facilitated by previously discussed protocols.

- Chat sessions can be established between two or more users using a chat client and a server. Real-time text typing and added features such as file transfers of data and audio, as well as voice over Internet protocol have been combined in the latest of these applications.

- Internet compliant devices are managed using the simple network management protocol (SNMP). This set of protocols is used for managing complex networks by sending messages to different parts of a network in order to retrieve stored data from SNMP-enabled devices. This data is then used to establish quality of service levels in a network. Hackers often use this protocol to survey a network's components and participants.

While there are numerous other protocols and applications that make use of them, the above are the foundations of the major use of the Internet by people and systems alike.

The secure use of these services is first predicated on the notion that previous infrastructures, networks, and systems that the Internet uses have been secured (i.e., telephone lines, cable, wireless, satellite, etc.). This is then followed by securing the transactions performed by the Internet services. What has been briefly discussed but not detailed is the role that security plays in securing the communications and services discussed in this chapter. This will be presented in the next section.

Security Services

Up to this point in the chapter, an overview of the telephone, cable, satellite, and Internet services have been presented. The shear volume of information that is transmitted and accessed through these systems is staggering. The protection of these systems requires the use of security services and mechanisms such as encryption, audit trails, and the like. A security service is a service that is designed to offset the potential loss of confidentiality, integrity, and/or availability of data or a data resource through the utilization of one or more security mechanisms and/or protocols. Confidentiality services seek to maintain the privacy of stored and transmitted data with the support of other security services and mechanisms such as encryption using a secret or public/private key(s). Integrity services seek to maintain the integrity of stored and transmitted data with the assistance of other security services and mechanisms in an effort to prevent corruption and tampering. The state of the data is said to have integrity when its content has not been changed by an unauthorized party. Availability is the capability of a resource to be accessible when needed, and as such, is the prevention of the interruption of a service. From these three concepts come the communication security services of authentication, access control, data integrity and confidentiality, nonrepudiation, and auditing, and will be presented in the following sections. These are the very foundations of securing information in today's data and telecommunication environments.

Authentication

In data communications, the use of authentication is an important aspect in validating the identity of a system or user. It is intended to establish trust between systems by verifying claimed identities in such a way that they are difficult to counterfeit. Authentication is generally used to confirm identities prior to initiating data transfers and/or granting access to files and processes. There are two-party and third-party authentication schemes. In two-party authentication, one of the parties wishes to be authenticated by the other party. An example of a two-party authentication in one of its simplest forms would be the sending of a user name and password by a client to a server. The server would compare the user name and password to its list of users, and upon a match, validate the user's identity. More advanced methods would include the use of a shared secret such as a secret digital key, that can be used to encrypt the communication(s) in such a way that only the two parties can interpret the content. In third-party authentication, a third entity acts as a trusted mediator between the two parties. This allows the third party to issue and/or manage the shared secrets of the two parties in a manner where neither party directly exchanges their keys in order to establish concurrent authentication.

Access Control

Establishing the identity of a party is the responsibility of authentication. Once an entity is authenticated, it can be considered to possess unique credentials that impart specific privileges to system resources. Access control involves the enforcement of privileges based on the system's access control policy. The function of access control is designed to restrict the activities that illegitimate users can perform, while granting access to system resources to legitimate users. The use of access control extends to the execution of system commands by both subjects (people) and objects (programs) in an effort to prevent a breach of the system's security policy. A reference monitor mediates every access attempt, consults an authorization database (i.e., access control list) to determine if access should be granted, and then permits/denies the action based on the policy contained in the database. When utilizing a reference monitor, it is necessary that it is always invoked, cannot be bypassed, and all accesses are mediated. It is also necessary that it is tamperproof by the subjects and objects, and small enough to be subjected to analysis and testing.

Data Integrity and Confidentiality

As previously mentioned, when applied to computing, integrity means that the data is unaltered based on its original state. Integrity can also be defined as data that has had no unauthorized changes. During electronic storage and transmission, data can be modified, corrupted, or destroyed through error or malicious intent. Also, the loss of confidentiality occurs when the contents of a file or communication are disclosed to an unauthorized entity. The underlying component of the data confidentiality process is the use of ciphers, or encryption algorithms that utilize the digital keys as process parameters. Through the use of cryptographic methods, data integrity can in most cases be verified before its use, and confidentiality can be maintained.

Nonrepudiation

A key security goal is accountability, which can be defined as being made accountable for performing some activity. A nonrepudiation service makes an entity accountable for their actions by providing nonrefutable evidence that an action took place by the entity. Evidence can come in the form of proof of origin, proof of original content, proof of delivery, and proof of original content received. The first two forms of evidence protect the receiver, and the last two protect the sender. A nonrepudiation service collects evidence in a manner that the entities cannot repudiate their actions at a later date, and retains that evidence in a secure manner such that it can be utilized by an adjudicator to settle any disputes.

Auditing

In order to perform an audit of the activities performed by subjects (i.e., people, etc.) or objects (i.e., components, etc.) in a system, an audit trail must be established based on a set of audit policies. An audit policy establishes what activities and events are to be recorded, and under what conditions. Audit services provide monitoring functions through the use of logs so that an examination of past activities and events may be conducted. Security auditing services are concerned with monitoring, recording, and maintaining security-relevant events so that in the event of a security breach, they can be utilized to secure the future confidentiality, integrity, and availability of a system. This includes the protection of the audit logs so that the data is not modified or deleted through unintentional or deliberate acts. Auditing services are usually coupled with access control services to provide a posteriori analysis of all the requests and activities of subjects and objects in the system.

Mechanisms and Protocols

The security services mentioned previously are enacted through the use of security mechanisms, approaches, and protocols. These security methods consist of symmetric and asymmetric encryption through the use of secret and public/private digital key exchange, as well as message digests, access control lists, digital certificates, and various secure communication protocols. These include, but are not limited to the following:

- **Secret key**: Secret key encryption seeks to secure communication between multiple parties, which each possess a shared secret digital key by encrypting the correspondence or content with the key. Upon receipt of the message, a party with the secret key can decrypt it and then read the message. Because secret key schemes use the same key for encrypting and decrypting, the keys used are not made publicly available. A server-based approach to secret key usage is where the secret key is used to create a session key for the communication session.

- **Public/private key**: Public/private key is used to encrypt a message with the intended receiver's public key and to send the message. The receiver uses their private key to decrypt the message.

- **Kerberos**: Before a network connection is opened between two entities, Kerberos establishes a shared secret key through a ticket granting server (TGS) that is used for authenticating the parties in the subsequent communications. Versions of Kerberos also have extensions to utilize public/private keys for authentication.

- **PKI**: Public key infrastructure is a key distribution system that issues, maintains, and validates the use of keys (Mazieres, Kaminsky, Kaashoek, & Witchel, 1999). The foundation of PKI is the use of asymmetric keys (i.e., a public and a private digital key) in the establishment of a session key. The public and private keys are generated in such a way that they are mathematically bound together so that either key may be used to encrypt, and only the other remaining key may be used to decrypt: even having one of the keys, it is still computationally infeasible to discover the other key from it (Schneier, 1995). While Kerberos, X.509, and X.500 have developed separately from each other, they may be used to facilitate PKI, and are discussed separately.

- **X.509**: To facilitate the identification and security of keys in PKI, a certificate authority (CA) is used to authenticate the public key by digitally signing it (Housley & Polk, 1999). This is known as a digital certificate. The validation and invalidation process (authentication) of digital certificates is handled by the certificate authority, and is governed by the X.509 de facto standard.

- **Digital certificate**: An electronic data structure that binds a public key value to the identifying information about the key's owner and is digitally signed by a certificate authority is known as a digital certificate. The certificate is used to assure any party using the public key that there is an associated private key held by the stated owner.

- **X.500**: The X.500 standard is a global directory service that is based on a replicated distributed database (Hardcastle, Huizer, Cerf, Hobby, & Kent, 1993). Programs access the directory services using the X/Open Directory Service (XDS) application program interface (API). The XDS APIs permit the reading, modification, and deletion of directory entries, while authenticating these activities. There are varieties of X.500 products (i.e., directory access protocols) available, and the latest version is lightweight directory access protocol (LDAP).

- **Hash product**: A hash product is the cryptographic result of taking a source file and putting its digital content through an encryption algorithm in such a way that the resulting output is of a fixed bit length, and consistently unique (i.e., the same file will generate the same output). This is performed through the use of a hash product generator that creates a unique bit stream (commonly 128-bits) that is based on the original file it was created from. Any changes to the original file will, with an extremely high probability, result in a different hash product being generated. A hash is generated from a message that will be sent to a recipient. The message and its corresponding digest are sent via some electronic method (i.e., e-mail, etc.). Upon receipt, the recipient generates a digest from the message using the same hash algorithm, and compares it with the enclosed digest. If the two digests match, the message has not been altered in transit. The integration of digital keys (secret & public/private) into the generation of a message digest known as a hashed message authentication code (HMAC) can provide an additional source of authentication and nonrepudiation (Krawczyk, Bellare, & Canettit, 1997).

- **IPv6**: The proposed standard Internet protocol version 6 (IPv6) is the next generation of IP, and will eventually replace IPv4 (Bradner & Mankin, 1995). This version is currently being transitioned throughout the Internet, and is backward compatible with version 4. IPv6 provides the following added features: an increase from the 32-bit address space to 128-bit; provisions for unicast, multicast, and anycast; an extension authentication header (AH) that provides authentication and integrity (without confidentiality) to IPng datagrams; and an IPng encapsulating security header (ESH) that provides integrity and confidentiality to datagrams.

- **SSL**: Secure socket layer is a security socket connection that provides a security layer at the transport level between the TCP/IP transport and sockets (Freier, Karlton, & Kocher, 1996). The objective is to securely transmit from one site to another without involving the applications that invoked it. The SSL protocol provides a certificate-based server authentication, private client-server communications using Rivest Shamir Adleman (RSA) encryption, and message integrity checks. The SSL client generates a secret key for one session that is encrypted using the server's public key. The session key is forwarded to the server and used for communication between the client and the server (Emmerich, 2000).

- **TLS**: The transport layer security protocol is similar to SSL. It is composed of two basic protocols, the TLS record protocol that is used for the encapsulation of various higher-layer protocols, and the TLS handshake protocol that permits the client and server to authenticate each other, and negotiate the encryption algorithm and cryptographic keys (Dierks & Allen, 1999). The TLS handshake protocol can authenticate both, one, or none of the connecting parties. TLS distinguishes itself from SSL by applying message authentication codes to the version information specifying the padding value, and by providing additional troubleshooting alerts.

- **IPSec**: Internet protocol security provides security services traffic at the IP layer (IPv4 & IPv6) through the use of security associations, key management, and use of algorithms for authentication and encryption. More specifically, IPSec enables a system to select the required security protocols, determine the algorithm(s) for the service, put in place any cryptographic keys needed to provide the service, and provides rejection of replayed packets and limited traffic flow confidentiality (Kent & Atkinson, 1998). IPSec may be used to protect one or more paths between two of any combination of hosts and/or security gateways (routers, firewalls, etc.). This is facilitated through the use of its authentication header and its encapsulating security payload (ESP), both of which are algorithm independent. The AH is used to authenticate the origin of the packets, and the ESP encapsulates the content within the packets (Kent & Atkinson, 1998).

- **SET**: The protocol used for secure credit card transactions is known as secure electronic transaction (SET). SET is the security foundation for most electronic commerce transactions by using digital signatures to verify and establish a secure transmission (i.e., authentication, integrity and confidentiality) of credit card information by merchants.

These methods are used to secure various aspects and transactions of the global information infrastructure along with additionally unmentioned protocols (i.e., too numerous to mention them all). There are volumes of publications that detail the above mechanisms, and others that detail their respective weaknesses and penetrations such as the book entitled *Secrets and Lies* by Bruce Schneier. However, security is big business. It is not in the security sector's best interest to reveal the inherent weaknesses in these mechanisms, and as such, the industry does its best to provide a measure of security. Even with this in mind, these mechanisms are better than nothing.

Security is one part mechanism (and the industry does a pretty good job at this); one part configuration and application of these mechanisms (not so good, as this depends on the supporting systems outside a given mechanism's control); and one part human implementation, intervention, and maintenance (again, people make mistakes and are inconsistent). It is not uncommon for many security mechanism producers to not employ a comprehensive set of security services in their products or systems administrators to enable the full capability of a given product (i.e., confidentiality without authentication for SSL). This is generally due to the high overhead costs of deployment, maintenance, and processing times for security systems, as well as the people aspect of overseeing and utilizing such systems. In addition, because networks tend to be independently managed and can be incredibly large and complex, they tend to have security policies and practices that vary throughout any given infrastructure. This allows small variations that may be exploited given enough time for observation and exploration by intruders. Therefore, when security is properly implemented, it may still allow for intrusions by those who are very skilled, or by those who are helped by the very skilled (i.e., exploits).

Final Thoughts of This Chapter

With over 500 million computers (according to the ITU) worldwide, managing, controlling and securing these systems and the networks they are plugged into is an astronomical task. With this perspective in mind, the owners of commercial and military networks have done an incredible job keeping them operationally sound. The efforts involved in keeping any modern system secure are dependent on all the supporting hardware, software, firmware, and so forth that is supplied by a diverse set of companies and organizations. The strengths and weaknesses of these products, and any interdependencies or incompatibilities between these components and systems, create a clear, heterogeneous environment, which users and administrators of networks alike must continuously learn to adapt to in order to maintain a consistent, secure environment.

Historically, with each new breach or penetration, manufacturers and administrators of systems have increased their security aspects in response to new threats, and have even prepared for future contingencies through redundancies and increased internal surveillances (i.e., intrusion detection systems). The current paradigm for securing systems is preventive mechanisms, followed by destructive testing by outsiders, followed by improvements in these systems in response. It is an endless cycle requiring continuous improvement. Therefore, securing systems requires constant vigilance and ongoing innovation. With this in mind, the global information infrastructure will continue to be exploited by criminals and terrorist groups alike as their penetration skills continue to evolve within this infrastructure. At the same time, users and system administrators will continue to learn to improve their defenses. Ultimately, widespread protective mechanisms, security policies, and enforceable security standards will need to be implemented throughout the entire global information infrastructure.

References

Bradner, S., & Mankin, A. (1995, January). *The recommendation for the IP next generation protocol* (IETF RFC1752).

Dierks, T., & Allen, C. (1999, January). *The TLS protocol version 1.0* (IETF RFC2246).

Emmerich, W. (2000). *Engineering distributed objects*. Chichester, UK: John Wiley & Sons.

Freier, A., Karlton, P., & Kocher, P. (1996, November). *The SSL protocol version 3.0*. Transport Layer Security Working Group.

Hardcastle, S., Huizer, E., Cerf, V., Hobby, R., & Kent, S. (1993, February). *A strategic plan for deploying an Internet X.500 directory service* (IETF RFC1430).

Housley, R., & Polk, W. (1999, March). *Internet X.509 public key infrastructure* (IETF RFC2528). SPYRUS, NIST.

International Telecommunication Union (ITU). (2005). *Telecommunication indicators handbook, Version 1*. Retrieved from http://www.itu.int/ITU-D/ict/

International Telecommunication Union (ITU). (2005). *Key indicators of the telecommunications/ICT sector*. Retrieved from http://www.itu.int/ITU-D/ict/

Jessell, H. (2003). *Broadcasting and cable yearbook 2003-2004*. Reed Business Information.

Junker, S., & Noller, W. (1983, May). Digital private branch exchanges. *IEEE Communications Magazine.*

Kent, S., & Atkinson, R. (1998, November). *Security architecture for the Internet protocol* (IETF RFC2401).

Kluepfel, H. (1993). Securing a global village and its resources: Baseline security for interconnected signaling system #7 telecommunications networks. *Proceedings of the 1ˢᵗ ACM Conference on Computer and Communications Security.*

Krawczyk, H., Bellare, M., & Canetti, R. (1997, February). *HMAC: Keyed-hashing for message authentication* (IETF RFC2104).

Mazieres, D., Kaminsky, M., Kaashoek, M., & Witchel, E. (1999). Separating key management from file system security. *Proceedings of the 17ᵗʰ ACM Symposium on Operating System Principles.*

Organisation for Economic Co-operation and Development (OECD). (2003, November). *Broadband and telephony services over cable television networks.* Directorate for Science, Technology and Industry Committee for Information, Computer and Communications Policy.

Schneier, B. (1995). *Applied cryptography.* John Wiley & Sons.

Schneier, B. (2000). *Secrets and lies.* John Wiley & Sons.

Additional Readings

Atkinson, R. (1997, January). Toward a more secure Internet. *IEEE Computer, 30*(1).

Bengel. (2004, June). ChatTrack: Chat room topic detection using classification. *Proceedings of the 2ⁿᵈ NSF/NIJ Symposium on Intelligence and Security Informatics.*

Brookson, C. (1995, February). Security in current systems. *IEE Colloquium on Security in Networks.*

Bryen, S. (2002, May). A collective security approach to protecting the global critical infrastructure. *ITU Workshop on Creating Trust in Critical Network Structures.*

Buda, G., Choi, D., Graveman, R., & Kubic, C. (2001). Security standards for the global information grid. *Proceedings of the 2001 Military Conference.*

Bush, G. (2005). *Executive order on critical infrastructure protection.* Retrieved from http://www.whitehouse.gov/news/releases/2001/10/20011016-12.html

Cerveny, R., & Stephenson, S. (1999). Managing technology of America's infrastructure. *Portland International Conference on Technology and Innovation Management.*

Clissmann, C., & Patel, A. (1994, September/October). Security for mobile users of telecommunication services. *Proceedings of the Third Annual International Conference on Universal Personal Communications.*

Ertoz et al. (2003, April). Protecting against cyber-threats in networked information systems. *SPIE Annual Symposium on AeroSense, Battlespace Digitization and Network Centric Systems III.*

Fumy, W., & Haas, I. (1998, November). Security techniques for the global information infrastructure. *Proceedings of the Global Telecommunications Conference.*

Gray, J. (1991, November). Information sharing in secure systems. *IEEE Transactions on Software Engineering, 17*(11).

Hust, G. (1993, May). *Taking down telecommunications.* Thesis, Maxwell Air Force Base, School Of Advance Airpower Studies.

Ingemarsson, I., & Wong, C. (1981, November). Encryption and authentication in on-board processing satellite communication systems. *IEEE Transactions on Communications, 29*(11).

International Telecommunication Union (ITU). (2002, May). A collective security approach to protecting the global critical infrastructure. *ITU Workshop on Creating Trust in Critical Network Infrastructures.*

Jacobs, S. (1999). Tactical network security. *Proceedings of the IEEE Military Communications Conference.*

Joint Chiefs of Staff. (2001, February). *Information security guidelines for the deployment of deployable switched systems* (CJCSI 6511.01).

Kent, S., Lynn, C., & Seo, K. (2000, April). Secure border gateway protocol (S-BGP). *IEEE Journal on Selected Areas in Communications, 18*(4).

Kothris, D., Beach, M., Allen, B., & Karlsson, P. (2001, March). Performance assessment of terrestrial and satellite based position location systems. *Proceedings of the 3G Mobile Communication Technologies Conference.*

Kuhn, R., Edfors, P., Howard, V., Caputo, C., & Phillips, T. (1993, August). Improving public switched network security in an open environment. *Computer.*

Lu, H., Faynberg, I., Toubassi, A., Lucas, F., & Renon, F. (1998, August). Network evolution in the context of the global information infrastructure. *IEEE Communications Magazine.*

Lunt, T., Kimmins, J., & McKosky, B. (1996, December). Security and the national telecommunications infrastructure. *Proceedings of the 13th Annual Computer Security Applications Conference.*

Nikander, P., Arkko, J., Tuomas, & Montenegro, G. (2003, October). Mobile IP version 6 (MIPv6) route optimization security design. *Proceedings of the IEEE Vehicular Technology Conference.*

Notare et al. (1999). Security management against cloning mobile phones. *Proceedings of the Global Telecommunications Conference.*

Notare, M. S. M. A., Boukerche, A., & Westphal, C. (2000, May). Safety and security for 2000 telecommunications. *Proceedings of the Conference on Information Systems for Enhanced Public Safety and Security.*

Papadimitratos, P., & Haas, Z. (2002, October). Securing the Internet routing infrastructure. *IEEE Communications Magazine.*

Paulson, L. (2002, December). Verifying the SET protocol: Overview. *Proceedings of the First International Conference on Formal Aspects of Security.*

Pei, D., & Zhang, L. (2004, March). A framework for resilient Internet routing protocols. *IEEE Network, 18*(2).

Peyravian, M., & Tarman, T. (1997, May/June). Asynchronous transfer mode security. *IEEE Network.*

Rabinovitch, E. (2003, April). Securing information technology infrastructures. *Proceedings of the International Conference on Communication Technology.*

Rejeb R., Pavlosoglou, Leeson, M., & Green, R. (2004, July). Securing all-optical networks. *Proceedings of the 6th IEEE International Conference on Transparent Optical Networks.*

Rozenblit, M. (1996, April). TMN security management standards in North America. *Proceedings of the IEEE Network Operations and Management Symposium.*

Sailer, R. (1998). Security services in an open service environment. *Proceedings of the 14th Annual Computer Security Applications Conference.*

Sheldon et al. (2004). Managing secure survivable critical infrastructure to avoid vulnerabilities. *Proceedings of the 8th IEEE International Symposium on High Assurance Systems Engineering.*

Siuda, K. (1988, March). Security services in telecommunications networks. *1988 International Zurich Seminar on Applications onto New Technologies.*

Stallings, W. (1998, March). SNMP and SNMPv2: The infrastructure for network management. *IEEE Communications Magazine.*

Swartz, N. (2003). EU agency will improve cyber-security. *Information Management Journal, 37*(3).

Swartz, N. (2003). Security efforts still lacking. *Information Management Journal, 37*(1).

United States General Accounting Office. (2004, May). *Technology assessment, cybersecurity for critical infrastructure protection.*

Varadharajan, V., & Shankaran, R. (1997, November). Security for ATM networks. *Proceedings of the Global Telecommunications Conference.*

Chapter V

Current
Cyber Attack Methods

Objectives of This Chapter

√   Understand that cyber attacks are not random but instead are executed with deliberate intent and specific purpose.

√   Identify many of the internal penetration approaches to achieve security breaches.

√   Discover the most common external penetration tactics directed against systems.

√   Come to realize the part that people play in the breach of systems.

√   Recognize that there are many components that are vulnerable to attacks that are outside an individual's or organization's zone of control.

Introduction

Cyber attacks are not unlike other attack methodologies. The first phase of an attack is reconnaissance of the intended victim. By observing the normal operations of a target, useful information can be ascertained and accumulated such as hardware and software used, regular and periodic communications, and the formatting of said correspondences. The second phase of an attack is penetration. Until an attacker is inside a system, there is little that can be done to the target except to disrupt the availability or access to a given service provided by the target. As will be presented in this chapter, there are many approaches to this end. The third phase is identifying and expanding their internal capabilities by viewing resources, and increasing access rights to more restricted, higher-value areas of a given system. The fourth stage is where the intruder does the damage to a system, or confiscates selected data and/or information. The last phase can include the removal of any evidence of a penetration, theft, and so forth by covering the electronic trail by editing or deleting log files. Ultimately, an intruder wants to complete all five stages successfully. However, this is entirely dependent on the type of attack method utilized, the desired end result, and the target's individual defensive and/or monitoring capabilities.

According to the CSI/FBI 2005 Computer Crime and Security Survey, it was reported that the largest losses due to attacks consisted of viruses (33%), unauthorized access (24%), theft of proprietary information (24%), denial-of-service (6%), insider Net abuse (5%), laptop theft (3%), financial fraud (2%), and the remainder is composed of the misuse of public Web applications, system penetrations, abuse of wireless networks, sabotage, telecom fraud, and Web site defacement. These percentages are based on the 693 respondents who were willing to provide financial loss figures totaling over US$130 million in a diverse set of key industry sectors (i.e., local, state, federal governments, transportation, telecom, utilities, medical, financial, legal, education, retail, manufacturing, and high-tech). These types of attacks occurred despite the fact that most of the respondents had security policies and mechanisms in place as part of their prevention and response plans. Just imagine the number of successful attacks that went unnoticed and/or unreported by entities that were not even part of the survey.

In general, today's cyber attacks consist primarily of:

- Virus and worm attacks that are delivered via e-mail attachments, Web browser scripts, and vulnerability exploit engines.

- Denial-of-service (DoS) attacks designed to prevent the use of public systems by legitimate users by overloading the normal mechanisms inherent in establishing and maintaining computer-to-computer connections.

- Web defacements of informational sites that service governmental and commercial interests in order to spread disinformation, propaganda, and/ or disrupt information flows.

- Unauthorized intrusions into systems that lead to the theft of confidential and/or proprietary information, the modification and/or corruption of data, and the inappropriate usage of a system for launching attacks on other systems.

The goals of these attacks can vary. Some are to show the weaknesses inherent in the systems. Some are political statements about the conduct of the entities being attacked, while some are about the theft of information for a variety of reasons. These can include target intelligence, internal process observations, or wholesale theft. As previously stated in past chapters, the perpetrator's reasons (i.e., why they have decided to penetrate a system) have a lot to do with the extent of the damages that may be incurred. They may wish to have a look around in an attempt to "case" the system, or may simply be looking for high-value (i.e., something that satisfies their penetration goal) data items that can be used for other internal and/or external operations. Some intrusions may be to do some damage to a system in that an underlying system or subprocess would be disrupted or modified as the end result of the intrusion, or as a step in a series of penetration activities. Intruders may also seek to change important data in an attempt to either cover their tracks (i.e., such as delete/modify an audit log), or to cause people or other processes to act on the changed data in a way that causes a cascading series of damages in the physical or electronic world. Applications of these concepts will be discussed in the next chapter.

The means (i.e., course, process, etc.) of an attack has a lot to do with the approach taken to execute the attack and its related characteristics. If someone wants to damage a system with a virus, then they need to consider how the virus will be delivered and what capabilities said virus is to be empowered with in order to create the damage done (i.e., delete data, monitor activities, steal intellectual property or identities, etc.). The design of an attack requires an appropriate delivery method and an appropriate device to perform the damage once it is delivered. Because an attacker does not control the basic choice of systems and protective mechanisms of any given network, they are left to choose from a variety of approaches that have both advantages and disadvantages for any given attack. At the highest level of these choices is whether to penetrate a system internally or externally.

Internal Penetration

It is a common fact that insiders can gain greater access to system resources than outsiders in most configured systems and networks. This is because certain service levels within a network rely on users and developers to be attentive to procedures, methods, and policies for the organization's overall benefit. Restrictions on users tend to reduce the overall capability of a given system. Thus, reliance on users to conduct themselves appropriately may lead to vulnerabilities, damaged systems and data, and future attacks. When it comes to access control, system programmers and developers ultimately tend to have the highest level of internal access of systems because it is they who create the hidden structures that provide services to users.

Periodically, operating systems and application programs have overlooked weaknesses built into their software. This is not uncommon, as pressure to reduce the time to market development cycle has created many dysfunctions in the computer software industry. The current paradigm of software development is to get the product to the customer as fast as possible with as few defects as feasible, and then to correct the software as defects surface. Would-be attackers may then exploit such weaknesses before they have been fixed. At first glance, this approach would be considered an external attack, except when the vulnerability has been deliberately created by those involved in the development process. Recently, it was discovered that Aum Shinrikyo cult members, the same cult that killed 12 people and injured 6,000 after releasing sarin gas in the Tokyo subways, had worked as subcontractors for firms developing classified government and police communication hardware and software. As a result, the cult was able to procure and further develop software that allowed them to track police vehicles. In addition, there may yet be undiscovered capabilities that were created as a result of their development contributions to over 80 Japanese firms and 10 government agencies.

This example shows that internal systems have an inherent weakness where users must rely on the quality control levels of the supplying company for their foundational security. In today's environment, people are forced to trust the secure operation of fabricated and prepackaged hardware and software systems. From this basic understanding, the following sections will be organized by some of the various applications and network software that generally exist, and are internally utilized by users and administrators alike in daily operations. More specifically, what will be presented are the software approaches that provide for internal usage with outbound capabilities (i.e., data and information can be transmitted outside the user's or company's system), and are frequently hijacked or utilized to perform an attack(s). Thus, an attack may or may not originate from inside a given network or system, but the execution of the attack is facilitated by the internal systems, such as in the case of an e-mail virus that does some damage but also propagates itself internally and/or to externally connected systems and recipients. These have been organized as usage portals, access methods, and deliverables.

Usage Portals

For purposes of this section, usage portals are application programs that comprise the bulk of a user's daily computer usage where they interact with the outside world. These include applications such as e-mail, Web browsers, chat clients, videostreaming, remoting software, Web-enabled application software, and a host of other applications. These and other usage portals are utilized by attackers to turn a system against itself, or hijack its applications to attack its host system, or other connecting systems.

E-Mail

It is said that the most ubiquitous application in use for communication today is electronic mail (e-mail). We use e-mail to write letters and send attached files such as pictures and spreadsheets, and depending on the e-mail client's configuration, it can even receive Web-page content inside a received e-mail. This particular usage portal reputably caused between US$3-15 billion in damages worldwide when a university student in the Philippines developed and released the Love Bug virus. Now this is no small matter when it is considered that hurricane Andrew (i.e., my name sake) caused US$25 billion in damage when it went through the state of Florida. Essentially, this small e-mail virus was programmed to infect the computer of whoever opened the message, and send itself to everyone in the user's address book. The deliverable was a virus, the portal was the e-mail client, the choice of target was anyone associated with an initial victim, and the damage was to distribute itself and then damage the host computer system. This is but one application of what a virus can do with this portal. Such viruses now are being used to inundate targeted installations (i.e., military, government, corporate, etc.) with tens of thousands of e-mails that are intended to flood the organization's e-mail server with more messages than it can handle while attempting to spread itself to connecting systems (i.e., a cascading damage effect). Because care is not always taken in the proper use of e-mail clients, e-mail servers do not always have properly configured filtering systems and users are not always selective in what they open and read, e-mail will continue to be a choice portal for conducting attacks.

Web Browsers

Web browsing has allowed the Internet to prosper and flourish by providing a point-and-click approach to informational Web sites about everything from basket weaving to building roadside bombs. With over 8 trillion Web pages, the statistical probability that some of them are designed to disrupt, hijack, or damage a connecting computer cannot be ignored. Built into a Web browser are the tools and scripts (i.e., small executable programs that execute requested resources such as Install on Demand, Java Script, VB Script, etc.) that can be turned against a user's computer. The same tools that allow a browser to execute the playing of a video at a news site, can be used to trigger remote executions of other programs and subroutines that can allow a Web site's host server to take control of parts of the visitor's system. These tools can then be used to read and execute files on the visitor's system in order to access information such as user account details (i.e., full user name, logon name, e-mail addresses, permission levels, last time a password was changed, IP address, etc.), gather previously accessed sites and files stored in the operating system and application program working folders, determine configuration settings such as version levels and the settings of the operating system and/or application programs, as well as many more details that are stored on a user's computer. In addition, by using executable codes that are stored inside a digital picture, malicious sites can make use of these built-in tools and execute malicious code when a picture is opened and/or viewed. Browsers also have application program interfaces and plug-ins to security protocols such as secure socket layer and mechanisms such as digital certificates that enable more secure browsing and communications. When vulnerabilities are discovered in browser applications, caustic Web site servers can be geared to take advantage of these, resulting in site redirections, server authenticity spoofing (i.e., deliberate identity falsification), and the installation and execution of malicious code. These issues, and others not mentioned regarding Web browsers, can be reduced or eliminated if a Web browser is properly configured and regularly updated, and therefore must be taken seriously. Unfortunately, the inherent design orientation of most Web browsers is geared towards an "open systems approach" for complete compatibility and interconnectivity with available Web services. This fundamental weakness makes this portal ripe for exploitation.

Chat Clients

Computer-user to computer-user communications is sometimes facilitated with the use of Internet relay chat (IRC) software such as MSN Messenger, AOL Instant Messenger, mIRC, and a host of others. Some chat clients allow a direct, dedicated connection between two computers, while others utilize a centralized server to log into and chat with others on the server, both in individual chat sessions and in the groups forums. An extension of this basic approach is with the inclusion of voice and/or video feed via a microphone and/or video camera. This combined approach combines text messaging, voice over Internet protocol, and videostreaming using software such as Apple's iChat AV. The vast majority of the products in this usage portal have no privacy protection (i.e., encryption, IP address obscuring, etc.), and are subject to monitoring, hijacking, and substitution of communication content attacks in addition to any relevant information that can be ascertained from a given conversation. Also, an intruder can use this class of software to obtain configuration information to remotely use a computer's microphone and video camera at a later date to see/listen in on the room that the computer resides. Care must be taken in the choice of software, chat server, and those who are to be chatted with when using this portal. However, the basic nature of people to become comfortable with systems, and trust previous relationships will lead to this portal being taken advantage of by technically savvy intruders and social engineers.

Remote Software

Remote software allows a user to take control of an existing computer or server remotely through another computer. This is usually accomplished via a modem or network connection. This usage portal is used to remotely manage servers (i.e., similar to Telnet), and access limited or shared resources on a network such as databases, application software, work files, and the like. Sometimes, the remote connection is completed in such a way that the user's computer acts as a terminal for keystrokes and screen shots that are being performed on the remoted computer using software such as Laplink or pcAnywhere, or the computer being remoted is actually a virtual, fully functioning desktop that emulates the look and feel of an actual desktop, as in the case of Microsoft's Terminal Services. When remote services are enabled and made available, intruders can use the modems and/or network address ports to gain access to the internal structure of a network. These access points tend to be user name and password protected only with little or no privacy protection (i.e., encryption), and therefore can be subject to external monitoring, and brute force (i.e., incremental generation of characters until a match is found) and dictionary password attacks (i.e., a dictionary list of potential passwords). It is this author's opinion that this portal is by far the least protected, and one of the easiest to penetrate when they are present in an organization.

Web-Enabled Applications

Everyday applications such as word processors and spreadsheets are designed to be Web enabled to allow the sending and reading of files and work-in-process projects between systems (i.e., integrated applications and collaboration systems). It is quite common to attempt to insert clip art into a document, and be prompted if you would like to browse additional clip art at the manufacturer's Web site. Other applications are integrated directly with e-mail and Web browser software as a result of being part of the same software suite such as Microsoft Office. Associated applications are launched and executed when specialty functions are requested. Additionally, many applications and utility software periodically check to see if an Internet connection is available and if so, may contact the manufacturer's server for update information and/or registration validation. Some software is still more intrusive in that when a connection is not present, it instructs the computer to dial or connect to the Internet without permission from the user.

Web-enabled applications can be used by an intruder's malicious code to transfer information about a system (i.e., via file transfer protocol, etc.), execute successive activities of an initial attack (i.e., transitive capabilities), and facilitate the spread of additional malicious code. Care must be taken in the selection and configuration of these types of software, as well as the source manufacturer. The use of shareware and freeware sources for Web-enabled software can sometimes have additionally built-in communications and backdoors that can be exploited by its creators and/or is the result of a poor software development process. It is one thing to have software with the ability to access the Web outside of its hosting system, it is another completely different issue when such software is designed to accept connections from the Internet without notifying the user such as in the case of many of Microsoft's Office products. Because users have been given the ability to integrate applications with the Web (willingly or not), the problems associated with this approach will be around for some time to come.

Updates

As previously discussed, the current software development paradigm is to get a product to market as quickly as feasible. When security faults become known as a result of this paradigm, patches (i.e., a software fix) are usually issued by the manufacturer. Whether the patch is for an operating system, utility program, or an application package, a process is required for developing a new patch, notifying users of the patch's existence, making the patch available in a timely manner, and finally, delivering said patch. Throughout this process, vulnerabilities can be created and/or bypassed by users and intruders alike. As an example, most antivirus software has provisions for updating the virus definition files to protect against new viruses as they are developed and deployed. Some attacks are directed at the virus software itself in that if the virus scanner can be disabled in some way, then a greater threat can be activated without the user being made aware of it. Therefore, updating the definition files and antivirus software is critical to maintaining a good virus defense. When the update process is circumvented (i.e., not renewing the subscription, disabling part of the update process, corrupting the software or definition files, etc.), a host of security issues emerge, usually resulting in a breached system.

With regards to operating systems and enterprise level software such as SAP, the update process has additional complexities that provide additional opportunities for intruders. One method of corruption that continues to be utilized is to send a system administrator an official looking e-mail detailing an actual, new security vulnerability, and providing a link to download the appropriate patch. This patch may actually be a piece of malicious code such as a worm, the actual patch with the addition of an attached malicious program (i.e., virus), or a combination of the two. Care must be taken to not only install patches in a timely fashion, but also secure the entire process. Since system administrators tend to be very busy, they may not take the time to check the authenticity of the e-mail, or the integrity of the patch itself before installing it. Even when an administrator is knowledgeable enough to not fall for this ploy, they may delay in getting the new patch, and as a result, not install a needed security patch quickly enough. The Code Red I and II worms, and others like them, have disabled as much as 25% of the Internet servers in one attack because of poor patch management (CAIDA, 2005).

Deliverables

With regards to internal attacks, what is being delivered has enormous implications for the results of an attack. The deliverable may seek to gain information on the intended target system. It may create a backdoor into the penetrated system that can be exploited at a later date for a variety of purposes. The deliverable may also be used to force a system to execute malicious code, or instructions to modify or delete data and other programs. For internal penetrations (i.e., internal usage with outbound capabilities), the vast majority of deliverables will be viruses, worms, and executable scripts (i.e., program instructions). Most other attack deliverables are external in nature, and will be discussed later in the chapter.

Viruses and Worms

Viruses have been plaguing systems since the 1960s. Essentially, a computer virus is a self-replicating program that attaches itself to another program or file in order to reproduce. When a given file is used, the virus will reside in the memory of a computer system, attach itself to other files accessed or opened, and execute its code. Viruses traditionally have targeted boot sectors (i.e., the startup portion of a computer) and executable files, and have hidden themselves in some very unlikely memory locations such as in the printer memory port. Like computers, viruses have evolved in capabilities. These include the ability to conceal an infection by letting an executable program call the infected file from another location by disabling the definition file (i.e., digital fingerprint used to detect a virus), by encrypting itself to prevent a discernible virus *signature*, and/or by changing its digital footprint each time it reproduces (i.e., polymorphism).

Worms are a type of virus that does not need another file or program to replicate itself, and as such, is a self-sustaining and running program. The primary difference between viruses and worms is that a virus replicates on a host system, while a worm replicates over a network using standard protocols (i.e., a type of mobile code). The latest incarnation of worms makes use of known vulnerabilities in systems to penetrate, execute their code, and replicate to other systems, such as the Code Red II worm that infected over 259,000 systems in less than 14 hours (CAIDA, 2005). Another use of worms that is less destructive and more subversive has been designed to monitor and collect server and traffic activities, and transmit this information back to its creator for intelligence and/or industrial espionage.

Trojans

A Trojan horse is a program that is intended to perform a legitimate function when it, in fact, performs an unknown and/or unwanted activity. Many viruses and worms are delivered via a Trojan horse program to infect systems; install monitoring software such as keyboard loggers (i.e., a program that records every keystroke performed by a user); or backdoors to remotely take control of the system, and/or conduct destructive activities on the infiltrated system. It is very common for intruders to make available free software (i.e., games, utilities, hacking tools, etc.) that is, in fact, a Trojan horse. In the commercial realm, it is also not unheard of to attach monitoring software (i.e., spyware) to a 30-day trial version of "free" software that reports the activities of the user back to the manufacturer with the consent of the user when they agree to the terms and conditions when the software is first installed. The notification of the so-called intended monitoring is buried deep within such agreements. This spyware can also be monitored and hijacked by intruders to gather additional intelligence about a potential target, and in this author's opinion, should be considered a Trojan horse regardless of the licensure agreement.

Malicious Scripts

Throughout the course of using the previously mentioned portals, a user will encounter the usage of scripting languages and macros that automate various calls and functions with connecting software modules and components. These scripts are designed to run in the background, and provide a means to communicate and execute legitimate code seamlessly between connecting/communicating modules and systems. These include Java Applets, Active X, and application software macros. Java Applets are programs designed to be executed within an application program such as a Web browser, and do not get executed by the user's operating system directly. This allows applets to be operating-system independent, and instead rely on the application program to execute the commands through its resident operating system. Active X is a combination of object linking and embedding (OLE) and component object model (COM) technologies that allow information to be shared between applications, and can perform any action a user would normally be able to perform. This allows applications to use Active X to eliminate the restrictions imposed by application specific formats for the processing and storage of data (i.e., they can be automated regardless of program dependencies). Macros are a series of stored keystrokes that can be sequentially executed at one time and repeatedly re-executed. This allows redundant tasks within applications to be automated and executed. Java Applets, Active X, macros, and similar scripting mechanisms have become a regular part of Web browsing, multiplayer gaming, and business automation, and provide a foundation for streamlining computing functions for improved services.

When the above technologies are used for executing commands and activities that are unwanted by a user, they can be considered malicious scripts. When Java Applets are misused, they can be employed to read the system properties directories and files of the user's machine, create a socket to communicate with another computer, send e-mail from the user's account, and a host of other functions. When Active X is misused, it can be utilized to instruct accounting software to write an electronic check to someone's bank account, and a host of other automated attack sequences. Macros have been used by attackers from their beginnings to perform virus-like functions, and as a result, have been dubbed macroviruses. These are executed whenever an infected document is opened. They reproduce by adding themselves to the application's "normal" or base blank document. Whenever a new or existing document is opened, the macro duplicates itself into that document. It is then transported to new systems when an infected file is transferred and opened on another machine.

External Penetration

For most people, system intrusions are typically considered an external attack where the intruder breaks down a series of barriers in order to move deeper within a system. Structures like the Internet and other telecommunication networks rely on hardware, software for users and computers to communicate, physical and wireless communication paths to transmit these communications, routers and gateways to control the flow and destination of the data being transferred, and service systems to make these connections and communications easier to use. The multitude of systems, subsystems, and components provide intruders ample opportunities for exploitation. In this section, an examination of the more common approaches to penetrating a system externally will be presented.

Social Engineering

When we were young, there was a standard notion that stated it never hurt to ask a question. If one is being polite, sounds as if they are well versed in a topic or environment, and can communicate a sense of purpose in their voice, questions asked in a professional environment can be used to hurt organizations and individuals by convincing them to disclose confidential details. This information, in turn, can be used for future attack attempts. The aim of social engineering is to get people to disclose confidential information such as user names, passwords, points of entry, working hours, and so forth, as the first step in penetrating a system. Traditional approaches to social engineering have included official sounding telephone calls from so-called bank personnel, or an intruder posing as an employee or system administrator, or even an official visitor using an employee's phone to call technical support while the employee steps out of their office for a few minutes. The knowledge gained from this type of deception may very well bring an intruder much closer to gaining an initial access point into an information system or network. Such information can also greatly enhance other methods discussed in previous sections, as well as later in this section.

Physical

The simplest access method to system resources may very well be physical access. Because of the small size of computers, it is not uncommon to have a computer server placed directly within easy reach for maintenance by a given department or individual. This is especially true of small- to medium-sized businesses that give more responsibility to individuals directly involved in using and managing the system. As a result, an intruder or visitor may be able to access the terminal while in proximity of it. This allows for the quick installation of software such as a keyboard logger, or a monitoring device such as a wireless transmitter attached to a keyboard or videoscreen. The information collected, by whatever means, can be retrieved or transmitted to the intruder for supporting later intrusion activities. Such an approach is not the only means that physical access can be used. Physical access can also provide the following opportunities to an intruder:

- **Primary unit**: The intruder may unplug a computer unit's peripherals (i.e., monitor, keyboard, etc.) and walk away with it. Once this equipment has been examined and/or modified, it may be able to be plugged back into the system and used for future surveillance and/or attacks. This is one reason why better organized facilities keep such systems in restricted, locked rooms, and govern the access of their facility by guests and intruders alike by enforcing security policies and alarms.
- **Cabling**: The physical cabling of an organization's network is another point of vulnerability that must be carefully considered. Transmission wires come in twisted pair telephone wire, coaxial cable, and fiber optic. In many cases, these internal wires traverse through walls and conduits, and eventually terminate at wall plugs, and/or switch racks or hubs. The ability to tap into these wires is related to their ease of access in the case of twisted pair and coaxial, and a higher level of skill and equipment in the case of fiber optic. In many cases, they are encased in conduits, but in many other cases they are openly exposed. Also, these wires eventually must exit a building, and as such, become susceptible to outside splicing.

- **Equipment disposal**: The proper disposal of older equipment is an aspect of physical security. Hard drives contain details and configuration settings of a once operational computer that was connected to an internal network. In many cases, these retired computers are given away to employees, or tossed in a dumpster after their hard drives have been reformatted. The problem with this approach is that computer forensic techniques, which are readily available today, can recover lost or formatted data on a hard drive that has been formatted up to six times. What is required is permanent eraser software that writes and rewrites a hard drive repeatedly, in a fashion that makes such a recovery impossible. In addition, old backup tapes and CD-ROMs must also be securely disposed.

Having physical access to facilities and equipment provides a huge advantage in gaining additional access to a system. User histories, activities, and data can be retrieved in a major step towards additional penetrations. Therefore, physical intrusions will continue to be an effective step in gaining additional access and knowledge by intruders.

Wireless Communication Medium

Wireless devices are appearing everywhere a landline, cable, or cord served the same purpose. Wireless devices utilize laser, radio frequencies, and infrared technologies to imprint data on its frequency wave as a means of transmission. These technologies range from line-of-sight connectivity as in the case of laser transmissions, radio frequencies as in the case of cellular phones and networking equipment, to satellite control systems and broadcast transmissions. The basic nature of wireless communications makes this transmission medium accessible from any point within its broadcast range or point-to-point path. This is both its greatest strength and weakness. Generally, when two devices initially wish to connect, a handshake protocol establishes the two devices' connection and/or any security mechanisms that will be used throughout the connection. This link is maintained until discontinued or interrupted. Devices communicating via a wireless link sometimes experience environmental conditions that cause signal degradation and/or data corruption that can result in the retransmissions of previously sent data. These two issues provide intruders with the foundation for piercing such systems and any security that may be present, or preventing the communication connection from being maintained. While there are numerous standards in existence for securing wireless communications, the underlying notion that the transmission can be openly monitored makes this transmission medium vulnerable to eavesdropping. This allows an intruder to observe and record communications for examination of content, security keys, and/or decryption of the transmission. Such communications are also subject to jamming devices that flood the wavelengths with "white noise" and therefore prevent a device-to-device connection. One last major security vulnerability of wireless devices has to do with having its source location ascertained. A transmitting device can have its physical location be deduced through a host of detection methods (i.e., triangulation, etc.) because all such devices have a point of origin for their transmission. While military versions of wireless devices have additional protective security mechanisms such as frequency hopping and spread spectrum, most commercial facilities continue to be shown as vulnerable to disruptions, monitoring, and intrusion.

User Access Points

Users of data communications utilize data pathways to access systems and resources on computer systems. In nearly all cases, users are assigned user accounts that specify the level and domains that the user is permitted to access. These accounts may be generic, as in the case of an anonymous user, or based on an access control list (i.e., a predetermined list of users and their corresponding access levels). The user traditionally enters their user account name and a password. The connecting computer then establishes a session (i.e., the period of time that a communication link is maintained) with the connected system. All activities that occur on the connected system are performed at the access control rights assigned to the user account. Therefore, one of the fundamental attack methods by intruders is to identify any user names and passwords to access a system. One method of achieving this information is through the usage of packet sniffing. As previously discussed, packet sniffing is a method of examining every packet that flows across a network in order to gain information on the communication content. When a sniffer is placed on an attached computer within a network, that computer may then anonymously monitor the traffic coming and going on that particular network. Essentially, a sniffer creates a socket stream on the network, has its network interface card configured to promiscuous mode, and begins reading from the open socket stream. When data is sent over communication channels in clear text form, reading it becomes quite simple. When a user seeks to connect to a system, that system usually prompts the user for a user name and password. This information is then entered and transmitted over the communication channel to the server for authentication. It is at this point that a sniffer may capture this information if not encrypted for later use by an intruder. The attacker can then gain access to the system with all the access rights of the legitimate user, and may even be capable of elevating these access rights once they have access to a given system or network. Because not all systems encrypt these transactions, sniffers continue to be an issue in securing user accounts.

Another approach that is used by intruders is to use direct attacks on the password of a user account. Sometimes, a user name is known or can be deduced from other transactions (i.e., social engineering, similar formatting of other users, etc.). All that is then needed is the corresponding password. This can be accomplished using brute force and dictionary attacks on the user's account. Brute force attacks rely on sheer computing power to incrementally try all of the possible password combinations for a given user account name. Dictionary attacks utilize the most common words that can be found in a dictionary, such as names, places, and objects, as the password for any given user account. Both approaches are typically automated using cracker exploit software. More secure systems provide a user a limited number of attempts at entering a correct password before they disable the account for a specified period of time. After this delay, a user account may generally then be logged into when the correct password is entered. However, many systems still do not provide or activate this security feature leaving it open to such attacks.

Another well-established user access point is the dial-up connection to an Internet service provider (ISP) such as AOL or AT&T. Throughout the intruder community, it has been very common to trade accessible or cracked user accounts for other software cracks and specialty exploits. Gaining access to such an account grants the user the capability to use the account for spamming (i.e., unsolicited mass e-mailing), anonymous browsing, penetrating other accounts without direct traceability to the intruder, and also the use of the account's access rights within the ISP. In order to check for e-mail, initiate a session outside the ISP, or other seemingly harmless activities of a legitimate user, the user account must be granted certain access rights within the ISP in order to view files and execute activities. These access rights, while restricted, are still greater than nonsubscriber rights and assume a measure of responsibility and accountability on behalf of a legitimate user. Use of such an account by an intruder may allow them to be able to view other subscribers' e-mails, access server folders and configuration settings in order to elevate their access rights, reconfigure various system components to attack other networks, or even turn the breached system into a proxy server as an anonymous staging point for other remote activities and/or attacks.

Firewalls

As part of the basic defense for intrusions within a system, firewalls provide an additional barrier against penetrations. Firewalls tend to be a combination of hardware and software that acts as a partition between an internal network and the outside electronic world. Essentially, a firewall performs two primary functions. The first of these is hiding the IP address of the internal network from any connecting telecommunication networks that may wish to observe and/or connect to a system inside the firewall. This is like making all of the telephone numbers and mailing addresses of a business unlisted. In this way, an intruder must first know the destination IP address before proceeding to additional steps in an attack. The second function that a firewall performs is the control of packets through its communication ports in both directions. A port is the end point to a logical connection in a communication path, and as such, can be set to accept packets that are inbound, outbound, and/or both for a given port. For instance, if a system administrator wanted to prevent files from being transferred in an outbound direction, then ports 20 and 21 (i.e., used for file transfer protocol) would need to be configured to reflect these wishes amongst other additional ports (i.e., there are many ways of transferring files indirectly). Firewalls are commonly remotely accessed using a username and password from a specified IP address in order to configure and maintain them. This makes them susceptible to previously discussed attacks. Also, because many firewalls are not self-contained systems, and therefore use a given system's operating or network operating system, any vulnerability that exists in the operating system provides a means for bypassing some of its protective mechanisms.

Web Sites and Servers

With over 145 million Internet servers, and over 8 trillion Web pages, security breaches are statistically probable given the open communication structure of the World Wide Web (WWW). The WWW is a system of Internet servers that support Hypertext Markup Language (HTML) documents. In addition to Web servers processing document requests from Web browsers, these servers use the user's browser as an interface for manipulating application data for databases and security protocols. As a result, Web servers and browsers are being exploited for intruder manipulations. The first of these is known as cookie poisoning. Cookies are small data files that Web servers access to identify a previously visiting user, along with any additional data previously stored within the file. They are also used as session identifiers for currently authenticated connections between the two parties. When a cookie is viewed by an intruder, it can be used to acquire information about a user and their usage history (i.e., transactions). When a cookie is modified or confiscated by an intruder, it can be used to impersonate a legitimate user of a Web site, and utilize their existing access rights on the server. Because cookies are rarely stored in an encrypted form, this type of attack continues to be an effective first step in improperly accessing server resources.

Another aspect of Web server operations is the execution of scripts. Initially, Web servers simply delivered a given Web page to a user's Web browser. As Web service demands continued to increase, new ways of processing data and user requests were developed. What was created came to be known as server side includes (SSI) and the common gateway interface (CGI). SSI commands are used for adding small amounts of dynamic data into a document. CGI is the standard communication protocol between a program (i.e., script) and a Web server. It fundamentally takes input from a user and passes it to a program. The program, in turn, processes the input and returns the result to the Web server. The Web server then combines this result with the requested document or output file. In most cases, these scripts are permitted to run with limited privileges. An intruder can use this limited access to elevate these privileges by executing malicious scripts that, in turn, upload executable files that can elevate execution privileges. From this point, an intruder may then gain access to a broader range of server resources for a variety of hostile activities.

As previously discussed, Web servers have additional applications such as structured query language (SQL) databases. Web sites use these databases to manage users and various activities such as granting accesses to restricted parts of a system, or operations such as permitting the transfer of funds from bank accounts. During the course of these transactions, servers make use of hidden fields for the temporary storage of data. These fields are linked to the source code that is used to execute these functions. As a result, an intruder who views this code can substitute new values in the hidden fields causing untold harm in the transactions. For example, by using a string command such as http:// www.sitename.com/index.cgi?page=index.cgi, the source code of a Web site can be displayed. From here, an intruder could modify the specific hidden fields needed to change the quantity of a transaction such as a funds transfer that is beyond a set limit, or change critical medical data of a given patient and the like. Once an intruder knows the database structure, they may also inject SQL commands on the database itself in order to create, modify, and/or delete user names and passwords. Such attacks continue to cause serious security breaches involving credit card operations, online banking, and other commercial and governmental entry points through Web servers.

The next attack in this section deals with session hijacking. As previously discussed, a session is an end-to-end connection between two computers. A session can be considered hijacked when either the user's destination connection is diverted or it is intercepted. In the first case, this is known as a Universal Resource Location (URL) obfuscation attack where a user is sent to a Web site that they believe to be a legitimate site. This is done by using a similarly named Web site or displaying the IP address instead of the WWW domain name. Another way to redirect a user is to embed an additional URL or scripting code into a legitimate URL address. This can be illustrated by examining http:// www.whitehouse.gov/homeland, which is a legitimate URL. When a user is sent to http://www.whitehouse.gov/homeland?URL=http://cybercriminals.com/ spoofedpage.htm they may only see the first part of the address in their browser window or the criminal's part of the site address may be in IP numeric form only. In addition, the insertion of executable scripts into the URL address by an intruder can be best illustrated by the following: http://www.whitehouse.gov/ homeland?page=1&user=hijack_script_code_file. In this way, a user may not know they are in fact executing some malicious script when they visit a given, legitimate Web site. This script may be placed on the server by the intruder prior to its execution.

Another session hijacking attack form is known as the man-in-the-middle. When a user attempts to connect with a given server using hypertext transfer protocol (HTTP), an attacker instead intercepts the initial contact and acts as the intended server. From this point, the attacker then connects to the intended server and acts as the user. In this way, the user transmits login information, secure layer initialization requests, and so forth, thinking the attacker is the intended server. The attacker then takes these user inputs and passes them on to the intended server, and thus impersonates the user. Not only can the information sent by the user be used at a later date for other intrusions, selected parts of the data can be modified before being retransmitted in an effort to increase or redirect the user's resources. For instance, a bank customer believes they are logging into an online banking system. They enter their user name and password. They then wish to transfer $2,000 to another account number (i.e., a one-off payment to another entity). Up to this point, the attacker has simply monitored and retransmitted the data sent. However, the opportunity presents itself to substitute another bank account number to become the recipient of the money. Since the amount didn't change, and the transaction receipt can be changed to show the intended account information, it may be weeks or even months before such a theft would be noticed. Additionally, the $2,000 could easily be changed to $20,000, given the initial account balance. Because networks can be tapped into at many different points, this form of attack is unlikely to be eliminated anytime soon.

As previously discussed, operating systems and applications periodically develop vulnerabilities that can initially be exploited by skilled attackers, and later by script-kiddies (i.e., attackers that download and use an exploit engine as the coded foundation of an attack). In the past and present, buffer overrun vulnerabilities have been packaged into exploits and used to force a server's processor to become overloaded to the point that it will shut down, or begin accepting additional commands that can be used to execute operations designed to provide greater access to system resources. A buffer is a block of memory that is reserved to hold data prior to processing. A buffer is considered to have been overrun when a program allows more data to be placed in the buffer than was originally designed to be processed by the memory stack. The simplest way to understand this concept is in comparing it to a deck of cards. Each card represents a space for program instructions to be executed, and are placed in a stack. Each card is then dealt into the processor to be read and executed. For a fair game of cards to occur, no more than 52 cards should be used, and no one should be able to substitute any card without proper authorization. When a buffer overrun occurs, the cards may get shuffled, misplaced, changed or modified, or thrown out and replaced with a whole new deck that may be "stacked" in favor of one of the players. Because software manufacturers continue to design their products in a way that does not eliminate this and other such exploits, they will remain a critical vulnerability in the future.

The last of the attacks in this section are known as denial-of-service (DoS) attacks. DoS attacks make use of the communication protocols (i.e., ICMP, TCP/IP, UDP, etc.) that are used for computer-to-computer connections and packet transfers. Data communication is effectively an open architecture, meaning that the contacted machine waits for some communication to be initiated by another system. In the initialization phase of establishing a session or connection, a series of data exchanges occurs between the two machines. The initialization is assumed to be consistent and mutually honest. When one of the parties is disruptive or operates outside the protocol rules, the receiving machine may continue to attempt to complete the transaction to the point that it becomes overloaded or incapable of accepting other connection requests. Essentially, DoS attacks can occur through the use of malformed requests, or by flooding the processor and/or network bandwidth with an excessive number of requests. Where DoS attacks become most effective is where a distributed base of computers simultaneously attack a server, creating what is known as a distributed denial-of-service (DDoS) attack. These complicit computers (i.e., corporate and home systems) are most often hijacked by the attacker in advance of the assault on the primary target by previously mentioned means. While the use of malformed packets for a DoS attack can be filtered out before they reach the processor, the shear volume that can be created through a DDoS attack is difficult to stop. Some of the largest computing entities have been taken down by DDoS attacks. While this type of attack does little to gain access to a server's resources, it does effectively reduce and/or eliminate the access of resources to legitimate users, and may disrupt a system to the point that it becomes temporarily vulnerable to additional attacks (i.e., knock down a firewall to access a server, etc.).

Routers and Gateways

Digital networks of all kinds rely on electronic switches of various designs and capabilities to transfer data throughout a given network and forward data to connected networks. The most prolific of these devices are routers. Specifically, routers are devices that forward data packets to other devices within a packet distribution system based on the destination address contained within the packet header, and a set of transfer metrics (i.e., shortest path, path capacity, etc.) that govern the load distribution of a collection of routers. Routers use protocols such as Internet control message protocol (ICMP) to communicate with each other in order to coordinate this traffic metric data.

Stored within a router is a routing table that contains a list of the IP destination addresses of all participating device nodes. Within a given network or subnet, routers advertise their reachability to other routers and gateways. Based on these two functions, an algorithm is used to populate a packet-forwarding table with these entries. It should be noted that a gateway is a router-type device that provides a complete protocol conversion between connected systems (i.e., border routers), and serves to unify traffic between two different network standards. For discussion purposes, a gateway will be considered a router with regards to attack types.

From the previous section on servers, the concept of DoS and DDoS attacks can be applied to routers. Because routers can communicate their current traffic capacity to other routers, overloading a router with more traffic than it can handle rarely disables a network, but it does effectively disable the individual router. This is because the path that it would use to communicate to the router that is continually forwarding the overload of packets cannot be accessed because there is no out-of-bounds communications channel for such a control function (i.e., the pipe is too full for a message to be received). Routers are also subject to malformed-packet attacks when they are not configured to filter out such packets. In addition, routers are generally equipped with the capacity to be remotely accessed from a preconfigured IP address for setup and mainte-nance. This makes them vulnerable to previously discussed password attacks when this function is enabled. Where routers become most vulnerable is when a router's forwarding table is poisoned (i.e., deliberate placement of corrupt or bad entries). This can be forced by an attacker through disrupting a router's link with other communicating devices, the replication of nonexistent links, and/or the fabrication of a nonexistent link. False router reachability and distance vector information can then be fed to a router, the router assumes that such information is valid, and in turn, updates its own forwarding table. While there are numerous proposals for establishing secure router communications, this vulnerability will continue to exist as long as routing devices continue to not have a secure means of authenticating communications from connected devices, and out-of-bounds communication capabilities for eliminating DoS attacks.

Domain Name Servers

Within the Internet infrastructure exists a network of servers that translate domain names such as http://www.AndrewColarik.com into IP addresses such as http://64.17.185.212. This is known as the domain name system (DNS).

Domain names are used for Web, FTP, and other related Internet addresses. When a user or computer uses a domain name as the connecting address, it is redirected to a DNS to acquire the equivalent IP address. This simple system allows people to more easily remember Internet addresses, and provides a seamless method for changing the physical server location of resources (i.e., IP address location) without changing the domain name. In this way, businesses can move their service support infrastructure without having to disseminate the change to the general public. This simple service that provides hundreds of millions of computers with perhaps hundreds of requests per day each, has become the central nervous system of the Internet.

The DNS system is a distributed set of 13 root servers that share conversion information between themselves and their supporting reference servers. When one supporting server does not have a current IP address for a conversion request, it polls another in the chain's hierarchy until a proper result is found. In addition, when a server is unavailable, the system shifts the requests to one that is available. This approach makes it extremely resilient to distributed denial-of-service attacks. This is best illustrated when in 2002, a DDoS attack occurred on all 13 root servers during a 1-hour period. Eight of the thirteen root servers were disabled, resulting in no noticeable service disruption. This is primarily because the system is designed in such a way that supporting servers rarely need to contact the root servers. However, individual servers are still subject to attacks that compromise the integrity of the IP address to domain name conversion process for individual requests. The first of these attacks is known as cache poisoning, and involves the polling aspect of a DNS server. Throughout the normal course of DNS server operations, the server sends out requests for the IP addresses of domain names it does not know. These requests can be responded to by malicious parties that provide incorrect IP addresses. These, in turn, are then added to the server's conversion list. As this type of attack began to proliferate, security measures such as the use of secure shells (i.e., SSH) were implemented to overcome this inherent weakness. A secure shell provides for strong authentication and secure communications over insecure networks for one computer to log into another. Thus, server requests would be protected against IP spoofing and source routing attacks. However, such protective mechanisms have their own inherent security flaws and weaknesses that continue to be exploited and/or used to bypass its protective measures, and as such, will allow clever attackers to poison the cache.

Another attack method that has been employed occurs on the user side of a DNS inquiry. When a user's system initially contacts a DNS, it assigns a symbolic placeholder for the address. The inbound response to the user's machine replaces the placeholder with the machine address. It is at this point that the user's request is vulnerable to spoofing and substitution, causing the redirection of the intended destination. This redirection may be accomplished without the knowledge of the user. This is known as a bind DNS attack, and generally occurs when vulnerabilities in operating systems and application programs are not timely patched. Therefore, such attacks will continue to emerge as software manufacturers fail to thoroughly test products before their release, do not provide a systematic means to warn users, and fail to repair their products via controlled updates.

Audit Logs

In the previous sections, vulnerable components in systems that provide security solutions and/or network services were presented. Many of these components keep audit logs of individual transactions that include the IP addresses of individuals, public and restricted access area transactions, user creation and password changes, and the like. These logs provide a wealth of information to both an administrator and an intruder, for the purposes of discovering areas of activity. Audit logs, when accessed, may be used as part of a reconnaissance activity for system attack planning. The primary value gained from mining such logs is the identification of network topology; its fundamental communication structures; the middleware platforms being utilized; and any security protocols being employed. Armed with this information, known exploits can be deployed to hijack processes and host systems alike. Because these logs can also be used by an administrator to ascertain an intruder's activities, they are often deleted and/or modified in order to cover an intruder's activities as an effective means for the removal of transaction evidence. In systems where such logs are not encrypted and access to these logs is not greatly restricted, intruders will continue to utilize the information contained in a wide variety of audit logs.

Final Thoughts of This Chapter

In this chapter, the most common points of entry, attack, and/or disruptions have been presented. The sections offered here, and their associated vulnerabilities, are but the tip of the iceberg of the available means at the disposal of an attacker. Essentially, internal attack approaches are extremely dependent on the state and the capabilities of people and their ability to use, configure, and maintain proper security in their daily operations. One means for countering many of these attacks in a proactive manner would be the implementation of effective security policies and procedures. These policies and procedures are a partial means for securing against external attack approaches, because many of the components and infrastructures are governed by other entities. Thus, the use of standardization in technologies and their configurations, effective infrastructure management, and the ongoing implementation of newer, more secure technologies is critical to protecting all users of these systems and connected networks.

At its very foundation, software, and its supporting hardware systems have an evolutionary aspect to them that is driven by market pressures and organizational financial accountability. Infrastructures are subject to the laws of economic reality. Newly purchased systems must serve their intended purpose for a period of time that makes their costs acceptable. In many cases, this means that changes in these infrastructures can take considerable time to adjust to new threats and existing disruptions or vulnerabilities. In the current technological environment, equipment and systems can become obsolete in as little as a few months, and tend to only be effective for approximately 18 months. Therefore, attacks on systems and their respective components will continue to be effective for some time to come.

References

CAIDA. (2005). *Analysis of Code Red*. Retrieved from http://www.caida.org/analysis/security/code-red/

CERT Coordination Center. (2000. December). *Results of the security in ActiveX Workshop*. Carnegie Mellon University, Software Engineering Institute.

Computer Security Institute. (2005). *2005 CSI/FBI computer crime and security survey*. Retrieved from http://i.cmpnet.com/gocsi/db_area/pdfs/fbi/FBI2005.pdf

Additional Readings

Alexander, D., Arbaugh, W., Keromytis, A., & Smith, J. (1998, October). Safety and security of programmable network infrastructures. *IEEE Communications Magazine*.

Anagnostakis et al. (2002, April). Efficient packet monitoring for network management. *Proceedings of the IEEE/IFIP Network Operations and Management Symposium*.

Bih, J. (2003, October/November). Internet snooping. *IEEE Potentials*.

Burge et al. (1997, April). Fraud detection and management in mobile telecommunications networks. *Proceedings of the European Conference on Security and Detection*.

Chakrabarti, A., & Manimaran, G. (2002, November/December). Internet infrastructure security: A taxonomy. *IEEE Network*.

Colarik, A. (2003, November). *A secure patch management authority*. PhD thesis, University of Auckland.

Crocker, S. (2004). Protecting the Internet from distributed denial-of-service attacks: A proposal. *Proceedings of the IEEE, 92*(9).

Dotti, P., & Rees, O. (1999, June). Protecting the hosted application server. *Proceedings of the IEEE 8th International Workshops on Enabling Technologies: Infrastructure for Collaborative Enterprises*.

Edwards, M. (2001, March). *FBI finds secret US source code on computer in Sweden* (InstantDoc #20178).

Ernst & Young. (2004). *Global information security survey 2004*. Assurance and Advisory Business Services.

Karrasand, M. (2003, June). Separating Trojan horses, viruses, and worms — A proposed taxonomy of software weapons. *Proceedings of the 2003 IEEE Workshop on Information Assurance*.

Magoni, D. (2003, August). Tearing down the Internet. *IEEE Journal on Selected Areas in Communications, 21*(6).

Mavrakis, N. (2003, October/November). Vulnerabilities of ISPs. *IEEE Potentials*.

Maxion, R., & Townsend, T. (2004, March). Masquerade detection augmented with error analysis. *IEEE Transactions on Reliability, 53*(1).

Nasir, B. (1994, October). Components, modelling and robustness of network management for telecommunications systems. *IEE Colloquium on Network Management for Personal and Mobile Telecommunications Systems*.

Ollmann, G. (2004, September). *The phishing guide, Understanding and preventing phishing attacks*. NGSSoftware Insight Security Research.

Pescape, A., & Ventre, G. (2004, April). Experimental analysis of attacks against routing network infrastructures. *Proceedings of the 2004 IEEE International Conference on Performance, Computing, and Communications*.

Reed, M., Syverson, P., & Goldschlag, D. (1998, May). Anonymous connections and onion routing. *IEEE Journal on Selected Areas in Communications, 16*(4).

Rennhard, M., Rafaeli, S., Mathy, L., Plattner, B., & Hutchinson, D. (2002, June). Analysis of an anonymity network for Web browsing. *Proceedings of the 11th IEEE International Workshops on Enabling Technologies: Infrastructures for Collaborative Enterprises*.

Rietscha, E. (2003, September). *Buffer overrun vulnerabilities in Microsoft programs: Do you really need to apply all of the security patches?* SANS Institute.

Sabeel, A, Rajeev, S., & Chandrashekar, H. (2002/2003, December/January). Packet sniffing: A brief introduction. *IEEE Potentials*.

Thuraisingham, B. (2000). Understanding data mining and applying it to command, control, communications and intelligence environments. *Proceedings of COMPSAC 2000*.

Voyiatzis, A., & Serpanos, D. (2003). Pulse: A class of super-worms against network infrastructure. *Proceedings of the 23rd International Conference on Distributed Computer Systems Workshops*.

Wan, K., & Chang, R. (2002). Engineering of a global defense infrastructure for DDoS attacks. *Proceedings of the 10th IEEE International Conference on Networks*.

Weaver, N., Paxson, V., Staniford, S., & Cunningham, R. (2003). A taxonomy of computer worms. *Proceedings of the 2003 ACM Workshop on Rapid Malcode.*

Chapter VI

Attack Scenarios

Objectives of This Chapter

√   Recognize that through global access to information, we are all potential targets.

√   Begin to understand just how much information that can be used against us is available in electronic form.

√   Briefly discover the vulnerable aspects and characteristics in our economic sectors.

√   Identify the connection between the electronic world and the physical world.

√   Come to realize the degree to which we utilize economic momentum as a competitive advantage, and how cyber terrorism attacks serve to disrupt it.

Introduction

In previous chapters, it has been presented that computer infrastructures tend to be large, complex, and generally interconnected systems on a global scale, utilizing a diverse set of telecommunications technologies. With networked computer systems, distance is not a deterrent in many of the attack forms, and their respective preparations. Because the sharing, accessing, and communication of data and information is a primary function of the global information infrastructure value chain, systems can be accessed from remote, cross-national locations through a number of means and methods. For a cyber terrorist to feasibly exploit the global information infrastructure and the underlying systems it supports, their understanding of each functional component of a potential target is required. This can be accomplished by performing a functional analysis of the target that is designed to determine the strengths and weaknesses of its defenses, as well as its operational structures and internal processes. This is achieved first through the gathering of intelligence on a potential target. Once this phase is completed, the intelligence is examined for the selection of *weapons* that are capable of damaging the target to a level acceptable to the attacker. An assessment is then performed on the potential attack methods available with regards to the approach of the target, delivery of the attack, and any resulting damage that may be inflicted. In this chapter, an examination of some of the possible attack scenarios will be presented, and also how access to information and systems help to further these attacks.

Target Intelligence

In the book entitled *The Art of War* written some 2,400 years ago, Sun Tzu states that: "He wins his battles by making no mistakes. Hence the skillful fighter puts himself into a position which makes defeat impossible, and does not miss the moment for defeating the enemy. Thus it is that in war the victorious strategist only seeks battle after the victory has been won." This passage simply means that through good intelligence and artful positioning, a skilled attacker can be most successful when their opponent provides them an opportunity to be successful. Because information systems are designed and maintained by people, these opportunities are likely to come to fruit given enough time. People are not perfect, and people systems reflect this imperfection (no offense intended). At the core of this concept is the means to gather information about a target, such as their transaction history, physical access and movements, schedules, and contingency plans. In this way, an attacker can learn critical details about a target before launching an attack, and maximize their effectiveness in inflicting damage on their intended targets.

Histories

In today's electronic storage world, daily transactions are being recorded and stored in databases for future usage, though this usage is rarely fully disclosed to the general public. The degree to which this information is being made available to anyone wanting it can be considered both intrusive and exploitative. The public and private sector's demand for information continues to grow. The demand for information about everyone and anything in existence is creating an environment where the additional disclosure of critically sensitive data is being considered a right rather than a privilege. The notion that we have a right to know anything about anyone or any entity for any reason is approaching the level of absurdity. The fact of the matter is that there are now thousands of databases that contain large parts of our daily histories, and are available via the Internet. These public databases contain the following details free of charge:

- Birth, adoption, and death records
- Child care facilities
- Home and business contact details of individuals, including latitude and longitude
- Demographics (i.e., population centers, economic details, etc.)
- School and college locations, populations, and individual degrees awarded
- Physicians, hospitals, and medical supply locations and contact details
- Church leadership and congregation records
- Political leadership contact details and schedules
- Court and criminal records
- Company registrations containing its officer's details
- Property ownership information of people and corporations
- Military personnel and group contacts

- Aviation navigation and pilot information
- Plane and train routes and schedules
- Political organization financial disclosures

With the proliferation of the above, private databases are also being made available for commercial use on a fee-based exchange. While many of these databases provide historical financial transactions, family histories and lineages, and so forth, for individuals, they also provide additional historic details of business and government entities. These informational archives contain enough initial information to select a high value target. It is this initial information that provides the foundations for further surveillance, and the probing of target defenses. Such information in the hands of a terrorist puts any potential target at a serious disadvantage in that they do not know the would-be attacker's identity, location, and/or specific intentions. As a result, they most likely are unaware that they have been elevated to the status of a target.

Physical Layout

One form of target intelligence comes in the form of the target's location and facility's physical layout. It is very common today to provide potential consumers with floor plans and property layout documents to ease their navigation issues and further presale understanding. Subways, train stations, airport terminals, shopping malls, museums, hotels, condominium complexes, city, state, and federal buildings are but a few examples of this approach. Facilities encourage the use of their complexes. When a tourist visits a city, maps are provided to ease their journey in order to facilitate such commerce. The open sharing of these types of physical layouts is a wealth of information for would-be attackers. The physical layout of a facility or home is extremely important when an intruder seeks to access stored information and/or any available resources at the disposal of the target. It is also important for planning a physical attack. With the physical layout of a facility, an attacker is provided with entry and exit points, the topography of rooms in relation to each other, as well as room capacity details and the like.

In Figure 11, which is available on the Internet, not only is the floor plan provided, but in this particular caption, so is the capacity chart for the amphitheater and technical capabilities inside the complex. Such simple infor-

Figure 11. Ronald Reagan Building interactive floor plan

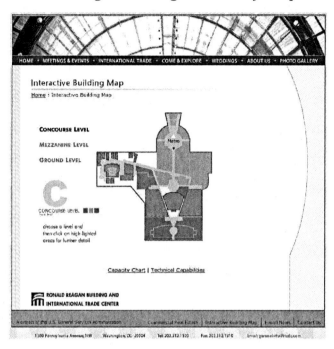

mation could be used in the planning of a hostage taking assault, bombing, or a host of other scenarios.

Emergency Plans

Most public facilities are required to provide some form of emergency plan in the event of a natural disaster, fire, structural development, or external attack. These plans identify what must be done in the event of an evacuation, and who is responsible for what coordination activities. They generally contain floor plans that map out escape routes and shelter locations. When electrical, chemical, and nuclear materials are present on the facility's grounds, these plans tend to detail their locations, and the needed evacuation distances in order to provide a safe distance from any potential exposure or explosion. These documents also may provide critical information about the local governing authorities that must be contacted in order to contain any undue exposure to the general populace in the event of an emergency. There is a growing trend to make these types of critical plans available via the Internet for whatever reason, as a simple search done on google.com will verify. When an emergency plan is made accessible online, an attacker could remotely modify or replace such a document in order to provide misinformation in a time of crisis, as well as using such a plan to amplify a physical attack with postattack activities. Imagine if an attacker were to acquire a city's disaster planning document detailing all the responsible parties, organizations, contingency plans, and communication channels needed to respond to an attack. The incremental damages could become considerable if the contingency personnel were initially targeted or response equipment sabotaged.

Schedules

Every organization and individual in today's workplace has a schedule. There are schedules for reporting for work, when to attend a meeting, break times, and when to go home. There are schedules for security guards as to when to make their rounds, and who is on duty at what times. Schedules are also used for running payrolls, performance numbers, and various computer batch processing and computer maintenance activities. These schedules are more often now stored in a file or electronic document, and are accessible to the individuals they are intended to manage. When these schedules can be accessed by an attacker remotely, they reveal who works with whom, when, and where certain planning operations take place, what individuals are in charge of various activities, and what system processes are executed and at what times. This innocuous necessity can be used as an initial step in identifying key personnel and organizational hierarchies to target individuals and departments for further surveillance and/or attacks, as well as when to perform such attempts. It also provides an opportunity to hijack various computer processes and functions, as well as providing a timetable for accomplishing such attacks.

Key Personnel

Organizations are collaborative unions between people. Within an organization are key personnel that establish strategic planning, operational policies, and govern daily activities. By virtue of their positions within an organization, these people have useful information to an attacker, and as such, may be targeted for further surveillance and/or exploitation. Key personnel are often granted expanded levels of facility and computer accesses, such as financial records, personnel files, and/or network administration permissions by virtue of their need for such access. By identifying these types of key personnel, an attacker can focus their intelligence efforts, as well as potentially gain control of critical assets and/or systems in their efforts to create harm.

Once a target (i.e., an individual) has been identified, an attacker may wish to assume their identity (i.e., social engineering, electronic credential forging, etc.) in order to interact with others to gather additional intelligence. When sufficient information is available on an individual, a terrorist may wish to assume their identity on a continuous, daily basis. Identity theft continues to be a growing problem on a global scale, costing consumers and businesses billions of dollars. For a terrorist, identity theft is primarily about freedom of movement and creating avenues of escape. Testifying before the National Commission on Terrorist Attacks Upon the United States, Laurie Mylroie stated that individuals like Ramzi Yousef (i.e., the convicted mastermind behind the 1993 World Trade Center bombing) may not be who they claim to be. Ramzi Yousef entered the United States on an Iraqi passport, and fled using a Pakistani passport as Abdel Basit Karim. She went on to state that Karim had previously moved from Kuwait to Pakistan, and that it is his Kuwaiti resident file that brings into question if Karim is actually who he claimed to be. Yousef's fingerprints are in Karim's file. The person's height and signature records do not match as well according to Pakistani records. She suggests that the fingerprint cards in the Kuwaiti resident file may have been switched by Iraqi Intelligence during the occupation prior to the first Gulf War, and as a result provided a new identity to a state-assisted terrorist. Imagine the damage that could be done by a terrorist with a stolen, domestic identity from the targeted nation.

Within Western counties, similar identity theft issues exist at lower operational levels. There are countless cases where criminals have assumed the identity of an established individual, obtained drivers licenses, credit cards, and even property mortgages. In other cases, these usurpers have committed felonies under the assumed names, only to have the real owner find that there are multiple arrest warrants issued with their name on it, or that they now have mistakenly created criminal records. Given a social security card, or similar identification, and a birth certificate, a new driver's license or state identification card can be issued by the appropriate authorities. These simple documents are the basis of generating an entire identity within most countries. Clever thieves have even been able to request duplicates of these and other documents, armed only with the publicly available information previously mentioned. They have also shown the ability to duplicate such documents electronically with the latest in desktop and multimedia applications, or steal the actual production equipment and supplies from the issuing authorities by breaking into a poorly guarded branch office. This makes identity theft extremely hard to detect, and opens the possible misapplications of an identity to destructive activities. The resulting damages to one's reputation and credit ratings is small when it is considered that your identity may be the one used to rent a truck that is used in blowing up a physical asset. Also, when a terrorist is armed with a new identity, they may even be able to take a job with a company that provides them with critical informational and/or physical access for the expressed purpose of executing an attack, and with anonymity.

Electronic Attack Targets

Attacks that target the infrastructure or underlying economic well-being of a nation state can effectively reduce available state resources, and undermine confidence in their supporting structures. One of the key success factors to any nation state is consistency over a long period of time. It is the continuity of government structures and policies that allow citizens, businesses, and other entities to have long-term planning with diminished risk. Such continuity allows for an economic and cultural momentum to be maintained, as well as greater focus on achieving specific goals. When a populace becomes concerned with the availability and consistency of services such as power, water, telecommunications, financial governance, medical, transportation of goods, and so forth, even the most simple of activities may not be engaged because of additional energies that must be redirected and/or increased risks. Therefore, when an enemy has superior economic might, attacks against these infrastructures are the next logical front in an ongoing war.

In the *Riptech Internet Security Threat Report, Volume II* (Belcher & Yoran, 2002), "The Power and Energy, Financial Services, and High Tech sectors suffered relatively high rates of attack activity, while industries, such as E-Commerce and Manufacturing suffered relatively moderate to low rates of attack activity." At first glance, these observations may seem unconnected to the war on terrorism, until several additional factors are considered. The first is that quarters three and four for the Power and Energy sector companies in 2001 suffered a severe attack 57% of the time. In quarters one and two of 2002, this figure rose to 70% (see Figure 12 for attack figures). When these

Figure 12. Q1 and Q2 industry cyber attacks in 2002 (Belcher & Yoran, 2002)

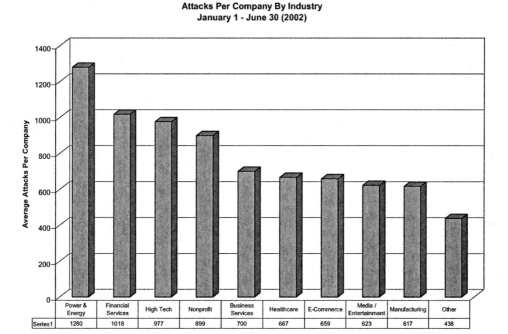

Attacks Per Company By Industry
January 1 - June 30 (2002)

	Power & Energy	Financial Services	High Tech	Nonprofit	Business Services	Healthcare	E-Commerce	Media / Entertainment	Manufacturing	Other
Series1	1280	1018	977	899	700	667	659	623	617	438

electronic attacks are compared with the declaration of war by the U.S. on Taliban-controlled Afghanistan in October of 2001, a simple correlation can be drawn connecting these two activities. It is one thing for, say, criminal elements to seek to penetrate financial institutions; it's another thing entirely when power production is electronically attacked, including nuclear facilities.

Similar occurrences have been documented throughout recent U.S. military interventions, and many of these have been previously presented. Attacking such institutions is not in any population's best interest, as such disruptions only eliminate the services that hackers, crackers, and cyber criminals require to conduct their trade. Therefore, such attacks generally fall to anarchists, competing states, terrorists' organizations, and their supporters.

In Symantec's *Internet Security Threat Report* (September 2003), it was reported that the top ten cyber attack countries per Internet capita, having between 100,000 and 1,000,000 Internet users for quarters one and two, consisted of Peru (Rank 1), Iran (Rank 2), Kuwait (Rank 3), United Arab Emirates (Rank 4), Nigeria (Rank 5), Saudi Arabia (Rank 6), Croatia (Rank 7), Vietnam (Rank 8), Egypt (Rank 9), and Romania (Rank 10). The vast majority of these countries have been directly impacted by U.S. intervention and foreign policies for decades. Despite that the U.S. government has established relations with most of these countries through regional and global trade agreements, antinarcotic efforts, and financial and military support; the general populace may not share their government's sentiments, and engage in remote electronic attacks on economic infrastructures and key sectors. These governments may, in fact, encourage such attacks by turning a blind eye from these activities, as well as providing the electronic infrastructure to perform them.

Public and Private Utilities

Power generation and transmission utilities, water supply and waste disposal systems, and telecommunications are primary targets for electronic attacks resulting in cascading consequences. These utilities provide the daily power, heating, water requirements, waste facilitation, and communication infrastructures for any progressive, Westernized economy. When these interconnected infrastructures are made unavailable, people, businesses, and governments can be deprived of basic services, and as such, be prevented from these services in times of crisis.

According to the U.S. Department of Commerce, in 2001, electric, gas, and sanitary services were approximately $222 billion of the U.S. gross domestic product (GDP). Coal, oil and gas extraction comprised $120 billion. Global electricity production exceeded 13.6 trillion kilowatt hours and 101.8 trillion cubic feet of natural gas in 1998. In 2000, natural gas accounted for 22% of the world's energy consumption (Quick, 2003). The physical distribution and control structures that are used to govern such infrastructures are vast and cover great distances, can be labor intensive in its basic maintenance and control, and involve extensive transportation issues. As a result, electronic control systems have been implemented to better govern daily operations, and provide critical data for load balancing. According to a 2004 report by the U.S. General Accounting Office entitled *Challenges and Efforts to Secure Control Systems*, control systems are vulnerable from the following:

Figure 13. Typical components of a control system (U.S. General Accounting Office, 2004)

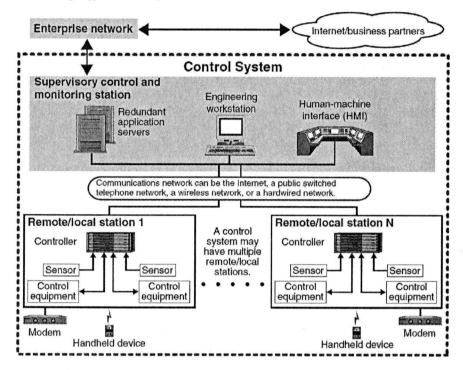

- Delays or blockages in the flow of information through control networks
- Unauthorized changes to programmed instructions in programmable logic controllers (PLC), remote terminal units (RTU), and distributed control systems (DCS) controllers, change alarms settings, and/or issue unauthorized commands to control equipment
- False information sent to control system operators
- Modification of control system software
- Interference with safety systems

Such vulnerabilities are a direct result of becoming increasingly integrated with business networks for business data, trouble alert transmissions between providers, and the utilization of shared public and private communication channels for the collection of equipment sensor data over geographic distances (see Figure 13). For industries managing such complexities, the connectivity of control systems is both their greatest strength and weakness.

With regards to the electric industry, power production consists of hydroelectric, fossil, and nuclear power generation. The basic components consist of transmission lines, transmission, and distribution substations that convert higher transmission voltages into lower delivery voltages, and control centers that use energy management and control systems to regulate the production and flow of power. At the operational control level, RTUs collect sensor data and transmit it to energy management systems (EMS) and supervisory control and data acquisition (SCADA) systems. Intelligent electronic devices (IED) are used to send and receive control data from connected devices such as meters, relays and controllers. RTUs and IEDs are used to issue management and control commands remotely. Fundamentally, communications between components and systems are facilitated via wired and wireless technologies, and transmitted over both public and private networks. The Institute for Security Technology Studies at Dartmouth College produced a 2002 report entitled *Cyber-Security of the Electronic Power Industry*. In this report, it was stated:

- *The sector has always contained security vulnerabilities, but these vulnerabilities have been compounded by the introduction of new networking technologies, deregulation and structural changes in the industry. Additional vulnerabilities have been introduced by placing ever-more energy management and control systems online, opening them up to remote access and linking them to corporate networks.*
- *Penetration tests and vulnerability assessments conducted by Department of Energy (DOE) laboratories and security firms have demonstrated the cyber vulnerabilities of energy industry control systems and related information networks.*

While the report goes on to state that attacks on such systems require a person to be physically present or have intimate knowledge of these systems to enact attacks, these EMS, DCS, and SCADA systems and PLC technologies and their associated standards are used around the world. Therefore, knowledgeable use of these systems is widely accessible, and foundational information can be acquired by attackers.

The other critical infrastructure in this section is the telecommunications industry. According to the Office of Technology and Electronic Commerce

(OTEC), as of 2004, there were over 651 million Internet subscribers worldwide, of which 24% were in the United States.

All of these subscribers are connecting through telecommunication infrastructures including residential and business phone lines, digital subscriber lines, cable, wireless, and satellite systems, and represent the result of an estimated US$1 trillion industry. With unprecedented growth, investment in the telecom-

Figure 14. Top 20 Internet subscribing countries (OTEC, 2005)

Rank	Country	Technologies Used	Market Information
1	United States	xDSL, Cable, T1, Fiber, Satellite	159 million Internet users (2002)
2	China	xDSL, Cable	53.3 million Internet subscribers (2003) 17.73 million broadband subscribers (June 2004)
3	Korea (South)	xDSL, Cable, WLAN, Satellite	29,280,000 Internet subscribers (2003) 12,719,210 broadband subscribers (2003)
4	Germany	xDSL, ISDN	39 million Internet users (2003)
5	United Kingdom		25 million Internet users (2002)
6	Japan	ADSL, Cable, FTTH, ISDN	10,272,052 Internet subscribers (2003) 13,641,311 broadband subscribers (2003)
7	France	xDSL, Cable	21.9 million Internet users (2003)
8	Italy	xDSL, FTTH, Satellite	18.5 million Internet users (2003)
9	Brazil	ADSL, Cable, Wi-Fi	14.3 million Internet users (2002) 200,000 cable broadband subscribers (2003) 983,293 DSL subscribers (2003)
10	Canada	xDSL, Cable	16,110,000 Internet users (2002)
11	Russia	xDSL, Cable, Satellite, Wi-Fi, Fiber	12-14 million Internet users (2003)
12	Netherlands	xDSL, Cable	8.5 million Internet users (2003) 2.5 million broadband users (2004)
13	Mexico	xDSL, Cable	10,033,000 Internet users (2002) 190,000 cable broadband subscribers (2003) 179,293 DSL subscribers (2003)
14	Spain	xDSL, Cable	9,789,000 Internet users (2003)
15	Poland	xDSL, Cable	8,970,000 Internet users (2003)
16	Australia	xDSL, Cable, ISDN, Satellite	5.2 million Internet subscribers (2003) 698,700 broadband subscribers (2003)
17	Turkey	ADSL	5.5 million Internet users (2003)
18	Sweden	ADSL, Cable, Ethernet LAN	5,125,000 Internet users (2002)
19	Taiwan	xDSL, Cable, ISDN, Fiber	4,779,000 Internet subscribers (2003) 3,004,000 broadband subscribers (2003)
20	Argentina	xDSL, Cable, Fixed wireless	4.1 million Internet users (2002) 121,664 cable broadband subscribers (2003) 113,336 DSL subscribers (2003)

munications infrastructure amounted to over US$200 billion in 2000 alone, and users placed approximately 36 billion calls (International Telecommunication Union, 2004).

Because much of our economy is facilitated by telecommunications, terrorist activities are likely to target this infrastructure for both intelligence, and in an effort to undermine the free flow of data and information. Such attacks also serve to create a force multiplier for disrupting relief efforts and targeted responses by government entities. Therefore, attacks that have occurred in the past, and can be reasonably expected in the future by terrorist organizations, may predominantly be in concert with attacks on power, water, gas, and other utilities that use telecommunications. These include attacks on police, fire and emergency communications; the monitoring and disruptions of voice over IP and E-911; and virtual private network targets such as brokerage houses' networked systems.

Banking and Finance

The banking and financial services industries provide the very foundation for a market-based economy, and facilitate the continued expansion and growth of the institutional infrastructures it supports. According to the 2003 *Encyclopedia of Global Industries* (Quick, 2002), as of 2000, the world's 10 largest banks had over US$7.5 trillion in assets. Japan lead the world with over US$4.2 trillion, followed by the U.S. with US$4 trillion in combined assets. Also reported in 2000, the world's top 25 banks had US$118.1 billion in profits. According to the U.S. Department of Commerce (2004), in 2001, the U.S. finance and insurance sectors comprised US$905.2 billion of the gross domestic product, excluding real estate ($1.172 trillion). This included depository and nondepository institutions, and security and commodities (i.e., brokers, insurance carriers, agents, brokers and services). The efficient exchange of goods and services is critical to maintaining such a system, and information technologies are at the heart of such operations. According to the Futures Industry Association (2005), in 2001, nearly 4.28 billion futures and options contracts were traded globally. This represents a 43% increase over the previous year, as new systems and infrastructures throughout the world made access to such instruments easier. As of 2004, futures and options trading came to nearly US$8.9 billion (Futures Industry Association, 2005). According to the 2003 *Encyclopedia of Global Industries* (Quick, 2002), there were "more than 37,000 credit issuers in operation at the turn of the century. In the United States alone, 200 million new MasterCard and Visa accounts were issued in 2000; a total of 185 million Americans used credit cards." The encyclopedia goes on to state that worldwide purchases made by Visa and MasterCard credit cards nearly reached US$2 trillion. With the expansion of the Internet, online banking continues to provide customers with account information, the ability to make payments and transfers, and apply for loans. Online sales of property and casualty policies also reached US$2 billion in 2000. Remember, the vast majority of these transactions are made electronically, utilize the telecommunications infrastructure (i.e., public and private), and are a key component in maintaining and integrating market-based economies.

Money is the foundation for sustaining any activity that has global reach. Terrorism is no exception. The state-sponsors, organizations, and individuals who have an interest in furthering a particular terrorist group's successes often provide support with financial contributions. With these funds, terrorist organizations can engage in both legitimate and criminal activities where the proceeds can be used to sustain their operations. In the 2002 testimony of Kenneth W. Dam, Deputy Secretary Department of the Treasury before the Financial Services Committee of the United States House of Representatives, Mr. Dam states:

> *Our goal is straightforward. We seek to prevent terrorist attacks by: (1) disrupting terrorist finances; and (2) following financial trails to disrupt terrorists themselves. Our first actions after the tragedy of September 11 were to identify known terrorists and terrorist entities, freeze their assets in the US, and work with our allies to extend those freezes world wide. Since September 11th, the United States and other countries have frozen more than $112 million in terrorist-related assets. More importantly, the actual amount of money blocked understates the full effect of the blocking action in that our blocking actions have effectively cut the flow of terrorist money through funding pipelines. For example, we disrupted Al-Barakaat's worldwide network that, by some estimates, was channeling $15 to $20 million dollars a year to al Qaeda. As another example, we froze the assets of the Holy Land Foundation for Relief and Development, which, as the principal U.S. fundraiser for Hamas, raised over $13 million*

*in 2000. Where warranted, we have also unblocked funds. $350
million in Afghan government assets that were frozen in
connection with the Taliban sanctions, mostly before September
11ᵗʰ have now been unfrozen for use by the legitimate Afghanistan
government.* (Dam, 2002)

Mr. Dam goes on to state that strong international cooperation has been
acquired in monitoring and freezing terrorist assets throughout the world. As a
result of these efforts, the U.S. Department of Treasury put forward a set of
recommendations for all participating entities that:

- Ensure there is appropriate customer identification and verification of
identification
- Eliminate the risks associated with correspondent banking activities of
foreign banks and other foreign financial institutions
- Expand the antimoney laundering regime to all facets of the financial
system
- Facilitate the sharing of critical information relating to money laundering
and terrorist financing

Remember, terrorist organizations operate on a domestic, international, and
global scale with cross-functional ties between themselves and self-interested
parties and/or states. If a uniform approach to governing and administering the
flow of monies can be established, then the expected outcome is that terrorism
will be stripped of the monies needed to perpetuate its agendas, sustain its
membership and supported parties, as well as provide the foundation for
supplying its arms and equipment. In theory, such activities should then be
rendered relatively limited.

One avenue that has been utilized in the past is the use of corrupt foreign states
and/or business entities to make available funds and distribute them through
their associated economic linkages, such as central banks and the like. While
these foreign transactions are now being made more available for auditing by
the Western powers, their true nature may still be manipulated and/or hidden
for at least a significant period of time. These funds may also be used directly
by the supporting entity to acquire supplies and arms, and then transfer the
purchases to the terrorist organization(s). Therefore, in truth, what these

antiterrorist financing activities do is eliminate one level of so-called legitimacy of such operations by removing access to public venues in the generation of monies. As a result, funding schemes for terrorist organizations must now be conducted through more covert channels outside governmental monitoring and control.

If a system is to be used to monitor and control activities, and freeze assets, then such a system will obviously become a target of those it negatively impacts. The very systems that governments are now putting in place to verify and authenticate identities and financial transactions may also provide a technosavvy or state-sponsored cyber terrorist with a vast amount of information on their enemies, and unfettered access to such a system once admittance is obtained. This is the true double-edge sword of integrated systems. In fact, since the invention of electronic wire transfers via the telegraph, criminals have been inventing ways of observing, manipulating, and ultimately stealing funds through electronic means. If this is not achievable in some meaningfully manner, then the disruption and/or destruction of such a system would become the preferred objective of any terrorist organization or state-sponsor such a system negatively affects.

Financial markets place value on products and services based on public demand and their associated perceptions. If such a system, or their subcomponents, were attacked in a meaningful manner, then products and services such as personal savings accounts, retirement accounts, and trade investments (i.e., stocks, bonds, etc.) would be perceived as having greater risk. The result would be less investment and usage of such instruments, and as such, diminish much needed capital for ongoing business expansion projects. According to a 2003 report to the House of Representatives Subcommittee on Domestic Monetary Policy, Technology, and Economic Growth on the efforts of the financial services sector to address cyber threats, the U.S. General Accounting Office stated:

> *First, industry representatives, under the sponsorship of the U.S. Department of the Treasury, collaboratively developed a sector strategy which discusses additional efforts necessary to identify, assess, and respond to sector wide threats. However, the financial services sector has not developed detailed plans for implementing its strategy. Second, the private sector's Financial Services Information Sharing and Analysis Center*

was formed to facilitate sharing of cyber related information. Third, several other industry groups are taking steps to better coordinate industry efforts and to improve information security across the sector. (U.S. GAO, 2005)

Because of the shear size of the industry, and the diversity of businesses and individuals participating that is needed to bring about changes, such efforts will be slow, incremental, and based on a consensus of willingness and capabilities (i.e., resources, technical, etc.). At the core of these efforts is the Federal Reserve system and the Securities and Exchange Commission (SEC), which have considerable influence over those entities wishing to conduct financial transactions with the United States. These organizations continue to establish policies and procedures that create audit trails and data security requirements of participating entities. However, efforts at the prevention of electronic attacks ultimately will fall to those participating entities, and so will the technical requirements and costs. Therefore, ensuring compliance of the entire financial services industry, as a whole, is a daunting task.

Because terrorist activities require funds, and these funds may well exceed the individual means of those conducting the attacks, alternative funding schemes through criminal exploitation of the financial services sector is a serious reality. The purchase of daily supplies, support communication equipment, transportation, training, bomb components, and so forth, all requires money. Therefore, attacks that have occurred in the past, and can be reasonably expected in the future by terrorist organizations, predominantly consist of usurped commercial and consumer credit cards; transfers of online banking account balances; covert account transfers from internal penetrations; disclosures of details for identity theft; disruption of financial transfers; and stock market DDoS, worm, and computer trading attacks.

Transportation

Modern societies rely heavily on transportation to deliver food, water, raw materials, finished goods, and people via land, air, and sea. This is often facilitated by an extensive infrastructure consisting of railroads, trucking systems, air transportation, and other transportation and distribution services. According to the U.S. Department of Commerce, the U.S. transportation industry consisted of a US$306 billion industry in 2001. The movement of

Figure 15. Coast Guard Cutter Hawser provided by DoD

freight via some 571 line-haul common carriers operating in the U.S. shipped 1.5 trillion ton-miles (i.e., movement of one ton of cargo the distance of one statute mile) and transported 9.5% of all intercity goods, as opposed to trucks handling 80.4%. The movement of freight occurred between approximately 3,000 stations and track terminals operated by approximately 15 large railroads and 600 small and regional railroads (*Encyclopedia of American Industries*, 2004). Amtrak reported that in 2004, it transported over 25 million passengers. The Air Transport Association reported that as of 2001, there were 19,306 airports, of which 5,314 are open to the public. Approximately 476 million passengers boarded planes, and over 4.6 million plane departures occurred. Air cargo in the U.S. amounted to over 12.9 revenue-ton-miles (i.e., one ton of revenue traffic transported one mile) for domestic transport, and 14.7 revenue-ton-miles for international transport. According to the U.S. Department of Transportation, over two billion tons of cargo is shipped annually by marine transport. In 2003, there were a reported 94.9 million truck registrations, over 776,000 bus registrations, and 196 million licensed drivers.

This infrastructure is large, diversified, and is largely reliant on individuals to perform their particular function in order to avoid loss of life and cargo, both during operation and in the event of some tragedy.

Because of the level of complexity of transportation systems, integration and control efforts have continued to be implemented. Throughout transportation system infrastructures, SCADA systems are being used to monitor and control component operations. In addition to the component infrastructure, the extensive use of commercial-off-the-shelf (COTS) products is utilized to control everything from traffic lights to air traffic control centers. The vulnerability of such systems is wholly dependent on their degree of connectivity to other systems, such as the Internet and/or private communication channels, as well as their physical accessibility. According to the Center for Strategic and International Studies (Lewis, 2002) the "FAA has 90 major computer systems and nine different communications networks. These networks rely on elderly equipment and use proprietary software that make them difficult for outsiders to hack. This may explain why the few reported attacks have not affected air traffic. In one reported incident, a young hacker interrupted local phone service in New England, shutting off a regional airport's control tower and the ability to turn on the runway lights. Although the interruption lasted six hours, there were no accidents at the airport. In other cases, FAA headquarters computer networks have been penetrated, allowing hackers to make public unpublished information on airport passenger screening activities, and in another case, a hacker was able to enter a FAA mail server." One primary area of concern is the use of electronic data interchange (EDI) systems, which are used to transmit and share data regarding passenger lists, shipments, orders, inventories, and the like. While these systems are not in control of electromechanical systems, they do provide a vast amount of information. Such systems are generally vulnerable not to disablement, but information attacks that are associated with surveillance and data modification. In particular, the removal of a passenger that may be on a terrorist or criminal watch list, the modification of transportation manifests for the purpose of shipping and/or importing supplies or components for further terrorist activities, and general intelligence gathering of potential targets. Outside of the computerization aspect of this sector (i.e., control systems and databases), which may be vulnerable to circuit control changes, physical attacks are the most likely form of attack. More likely is the potential for terrorists to identify a high-value target electronically, and then launch the physical attack against such targets as chemical transports, petroleum store houses, hazardous material shipments, and/or against passengers of transport services.

Figure 16. Operating room provided by DoD

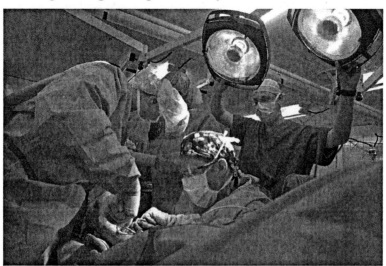

Medical

At the time of writing this book, the U.S. Census Bureau reported that there are approximately 295 million people living in the U.S. and over 6.4 billion in the world. According to the National Center for Health Statistics (2004), U.S. healthcare expenditures in 2002 totaled US$1.6 trillion, or 14.9% of GDP, which is the highest of all nations. This includes hospitals, medical practices, Health Maintenance Organizations (HMOs), pharmacies, emergency medical services, and medical and governmental insurance programs. In order to efficiently administer and treat people, databases are employed at all levels of the industry. This includes the local medical practitioners, pharmacies, emergency medical centers and ambulance services, hospitals, group care administrations, insurance companies, and governmental insurance programs such as Medicare and Medicaid. These databases contain enough information on individuals for a terrorist to search for an appropriate target or targets, and proceed with a wide variety of attack options. These attacks may include the modification of critical medical information such as blood type, immunization history, and/or acting on any confidential disease details. The modification of such details could cause the medical practitioners to diagnose a course of treatment that could be fatal to the patient. There may also be sufficient information contained in such databases that the identity of a person could be assumed with little difficulty, as previously presented.

Another critical area of such systems is the potential for inventory-level manipulation and shelf life reordering of life-saving antidotes and medical supplies reserved in the event of a chemical, biological, or nuclear attack. The modification of such data would seriously hamper response team efforts to treat victims after such an attack, and amplify the loss of life that may result. Also, such database access may provide storage information of contagions that may be later acquired by terrorists, and used against a given population. This is of primary importance in medical facilities that conduct research on contagion prevention and vaccination.

In an attempt to standardize and simplify the healthcare administration process throughout the U.S., the Health Insurance Portability and Accountability Act of 1996 (HIPAA) was passed, by Congress, as an initial step to reform the insurance market. One of the main goals of HIPAA was to reduce administrative costs in the healthcare industry by requiring the use of electronic transmission of administrative and financial data in a standardized form. In particular, HIPAA outlines the simplification of the billing and claims process via computer systems and electronic communications (i.e., EDI), as well as the details of patients' records containing information about medical conditions and status in a uniform manner, regardless of a healthcare provider's proprietary system. One provision of electronic storage and transmission of patient information is the security aspect of such systems. This requirement is placed solely on the health plans, clearinghouses, and providers to ensure the integrity and confidentiality of the records at all phases of the process. Such a requirement to produce an all-electronic communication structure, while requiring security, places healthcare providers in a bi-polar predicament (i.e., provide all information and provide privacy). In addition, when the size and complexity of this industry is considered regarding the standardization of electronic security, the reality surfaces that such standards will be geared towards individualized healthcare providers, because each has a different system performing different operations in a proprietary manner. What this means in the practical sense is that the U.S. medical electronic infrastructure now contains vast amounts of standardized data that is subject to external eavesdropping of EDI transfers by a host of potential attackers, amongst a host of other issues.

Education

As of 2003, according to the National Center for Education Statistics (2004), there were over 70 million people enrolled in U.S. schools (54 million) and colleges (16 million), and over 4 million people were employed as school teachers and college faculty. The major issues that exist within the U.S. education sector are Internet connectivity and its access to information resources, and the predominance of foreign nationals to immigrate for the purpose of attending educational institutions. The first of these issues that will be presented is the composition of connectivity. According to the National Center for Education Statistics (2004), it was reported in 2002 that:

- *94 percent of public schools with Internet access used broad-band connections to access the Internet,*
- *of the schools using Internet connections, 88 percent indicated that they used broadband wireless Internet connections,*
- *15 percent of all public school instructional rooms had wireless Internet connections.*

The extent by which schools are connected to the global information infrastructure allows students at all levels to have access to research databases and library resources in most disciplines, communicate and interact with fellow students regardless of geographic distances, and acquire advanced knowledge and skills in technical and scientific areas. In fact, the expansion and continued integration of Internet connectivity has become a critical component in educational instruction (see Figure 17).

With this proliferation comes the necessity to assign students with user accounts that have varying degrees of access control rights and user capabilities, such as e-mail, FTP, and the like. In most cases, the computers that are used by students are publicly accessed in designated areas (i.e., meaning multiple users on a single computer). This provides for a host of attacks (i.e., electronic and social) that may be employed to gain access to fellow students' accounts for anonymous communications and resource searches. The most relevant example of this is the use of Nicholas Berg's 1999 account by Zacarias Moussaoui in Norman, Oklahoma, where the accused terrorist used a fellow student's account for a number of undisclosed activities.

The second primary issue that applies to the education sector is the increasing levels of foreign nationals studying and teaching at U.S. schools. In a 2002 paper written by Professor George Borjas entitled *Rethinking foreign students: A question of national interest,* he states that over a 29-year period, the State Department went from issuing 65,000 student visas to 315,000 by

Figure 17. Internet enabled instructional rooms (NCES, 2003)

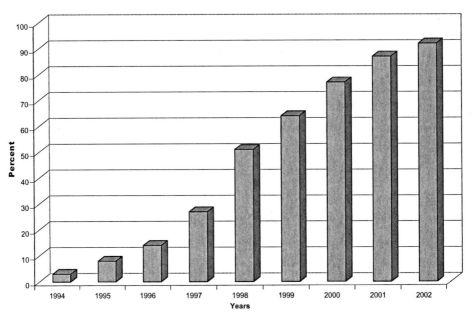

Public Schools with Internet Enabled Instructional Rooms

2000. The ability to abuse such a privilege is embodied by Hani Hasan Hanjour, who received a student visa to study English at ELS Language Centers. Instead of attending a single class, he entered the U.S. in order to be one of the terrorists that crashed a jetliner into the Pentagon on September 11th. It has been estimated that there are approximately 1 million foreign students residing in the U.S. attending all levels of undergraduate and graduate degree programs, and these students, once inside the U.S., can be difficult to monitor and track.

An associated issue with restricting and controlling visas to foreign nationals is that many legitimate foreign students return to their home countries with a positive understanding of the American culture and business processes, and tend to obtain higher levels of authority within their respective countries. For those students that obtain permanent residence after obtaining their degrees, most go on to be contributing members of American society. Therefore, any restrictions to this venue may seriously hinder future U.S. relations. To prevent such an outcome, education facilities must instead focus on policies and procedures that help to prevent the abuse of facilities and electronic resources. The aspect of immigration controls, while important, must fall outside this particular discussion.

Government

The United States government is comprised of multiple branches, departments, and agencies. The scope and depth of governmental integration into American society far exceeds the size of this book. Everything from customs and immigration services, taxation and social programs, law enforcement and the judicial, to military operations and national defense are managed and/or facilitated by local, state, and federal employees. According to the U.S. Department of Commerce (2004), government spending comprised approximately 19.7% of the GDP in 2002. This is composed of 23% for federal and 77% for state and local government expenditures. Where government expenditures are concerned, audit trails detailing people and transactions are prolific. This information is now being stored in government databases and document archives in searchable forms that, until recently, could only be accessed by selected agencies via the Intelligence Community System for Information Sharing (ICSIS), which is a Web-based system that combines the Top Secret Joint Worldwide Intelligence Communication System (JWICS) and the Secret Internet Protocol Routing Network (SIPRNET).

The government's influence, size, and complexity has not been overlooked by individual citizens, officials, or the terrorists themselves. In an effort to better organize and administer governmental efforts to defend itself and its citizens, a massive consolidation of agencies and departments is being organized under the U.S. Department of Homeland Security. The coordination of these multiple agencies and departments will continue to be under presidential control, with the main goal of aligning similar functions across multiple agencies. It has been suggested that such a consolidation will provide improved preparation and rapid response to disasters and terrorist attacks, through increased border and transportation security, and infrastructure protection, including physical assets, telecommunications, and cyber security. As an additional step towards information unification, the Director of National Intelligence was legislated through the Intelligence Reform and Terrorism Prevention Act of 2004. This office was created for the centralization of the gathering, sharing, and analysis of intelligence, both domestic and international. This new directorship is designed to reorganize and improve the management of the national intelligence community, including the joint operational coordination procedures between the Department of Defense and the Central Intelligence Agency. This legislation provides for additional requirements for increased cooperation and intelligence sharing between departments and agencies. While these efforts may produce long-

Figure 18. Interoperability tests provided by Kristin Ruleau

term results, it is the opinion of this author that such a massive consolidation of people, resources, and power is easily a decade away from any tangible results. Organizational culture has its own momentum that requires time to adjust to structural change, and the speed of this change is dependent on the degree of cooperation that can be obtained by federal agencies doing the job and legislative committees pulling the purse strings.

On a state and municipal level, governmental efforts are less prepared for the threat of cyber terrorism. It was reported by the National League of Cities that: "only 43 percent of large cities and 26 percent of all cities have developed strategies to address cyber terrorism." This is despite the fact that a series of congressional hearings over the last several years have occurred that clearly enunciate this emerging threat. These organizations have the same, if not more detailed information on its residents, as well as the details of the state of local businesses as to compliance with police, fire, and safety inspection officials.

Administrative government is not the only target for electronic attacks. A key military objective is to achieve information superiority, and the U.S. armed forces is no exception. In fact, the U.S. military is one of the most advanced, high-tech structures in existence, comprising the coordination, supply, and deployment of over 1.4 million troops world-wide, not to mention hundreds of billions of dollars in assets. As part of the Department of Defense's efforts to modernize and evolve the military, a transition from platform-centric to network-centric warfare is being implemented aggressively in order to change the battle space. In his welcoming address at the Naval War College Symposium on Computer Network "Attack" and International Law in 1999, Vice Admiral Cebrowski stated "Network-Centric Warfare enables a shift from attrition-based warfare to a much faster and effects-based warfighting style, one characterized not only by operating inside an opponent's decision loop by speed of command, but by an ability to change the warfare context or ecosystem." He further went on to state that: "a core strategic goal must be to design, build, and operate secure IT systems-resistant to Computer Network Exploitation and Computer Network Attack. Disruption or corruption of these systems could have devastating strategic effects." Disruptions, interceptions, and/or modifications of military information would seriously undermine its command and control functions, as well as its preparedness and logistical support for operations.

Therefore, one of the military's greatest assets may also become one of its greatest weaknesses. One technical reason that military networks are currently subject to attack is that they heavily rely on and utilize commercial communication pathways and services. Many of these systems and infrastructures are functionally outside the government's and military's control, and therefore, will continue to be the focus of electronic attacks.

Precursor to a Physical Attack

The last aspect in this chapter is the realization of the preceding sections and chapters. Somewhere in perhaps the United Arab Emirates, Iran, and/or Malaysia, there are technical computer specialists working towards mastery of the global information infrastructure. Perhaps instead of a few selected people, teams are assembled that slowly progress their individual skills, aptitudes and agendas, operating in a distributed, geographically dispersed manner. Their goals are, in their own minds, very simple: to bring down high-value targets that represent Western power and so-called Western aggression over Muslims or some other repressed peoples throughout third-world nations. Perhaps this target will be a regional power grid or the stock exchange. Anything that relies on a computer network infrastructure for its continued operations, and facilitates the economic and military might of the Western powers. They will have worked hard to build a cyber task force that shares its knowledge, focuses their respective efforts, and coordinates the execution of its members' plans. Throughout this progression, each individual is charged with the creation and maintenance of disseminating their respective group's activities, accomplishments, recruitment, and training materials. These individuals are responsible for training the devoted as to how to transport and communicate the group's data and information in a secure manner, acquire details on high-value targets from both without and within their secured networks, assemble dossiers for its leadership's review, and devise attacks that will maximize fear and panic in the enemy's citizens in order to undermine so-called free societies.

As part of their reconnaissance, these resourceful individuals may begin by tapping the communication lines of civilian and military network infrastructures, simply gathering the details of communications. They may explore the use of such data by casual use of user accounts and passwords to provide alternative communication channels for group communications. They may use captured account details to send unwarranted SPAM e-mails containing Trojan horses, or commercially available backdoor software. They may simply accumulate extensive dossiers on individuals that are ripe for identity theft, and therefore provide the means for group members to operate without repercussions, and provide ease of movement throughout a host of nations. These individuals may also be identified as feasible targets for kidnapping, murder, and extortion schemes. There are many motivational forms of terrorism, and the term high-value target has many associated meanings. Because terrorism has a political component, enacting change by showing how vulnerable public officials and wealthy parties are becomes a real weapon in the global media environment for a terrorist. They may then wish to seize the digital broadcast lines of the media for inserting their own perspectives on regular viewers in defense of their actions. The list of opportunities is as vast as any well-organized business or government operation.

As their learning curve diminishes, their mastery and acquired knowledge will permit these individuals and groups to selectively, precisely target physical assets for attack. As a precursor to such attacks, their likelihood of success greatly increases, as does their likelihood of amplifying the devastation effects. Imagine if mobile phone users had not been alerted on the flight over Pennsylvania on September 11th, or emergency response teams and hospitals had no means of coordinating rescue and relief efforts: just how much more fear, damage and trauma may have occurred. Imagine for a moment if an electromagnetic pulse (EMP) bomb was set off moments before a building is blown up. Such a pulse would disable computer networks within its blast radius, shutting down critical telecommunications, power, water, and transportation systems resulting in mass confusion and gridlock. Then, when a physical attack occurs shortly thereafter, the disaster is only made worse. Such is the raw potential to attack individuals, organizations, infrastructures, and key economic sectors in a modern, digital world.

Final Thoughts of This Chapter

Theorists sometimes view the world in the micro and the macro in order to get a different perspective as to how these two categories progress and interact with each other. On the macro level, individuals and small groups and organizations tend to create rhythms in their daily lives that carry them through the highs and lows of normal current events. They are vulnerable to being exploited and/or attacked directly by cyber terrorists. They also, on a collective level, inherently create the macro. Large groups and key sectors have a degree of synergy that moves in a collective direction and momentum. The micro and the macro sustain each other in a symbiotic relationship. When a large enough percentage of individuals and or small groups (i.e., the micro) are impacted by terrorist activities, the collective becomes affected as a secondary consequence. When the large groups and key sectors (i.e., the macro) are impacted by terrorist activities, the individuals that comprise them are forced to operate differently. The two are interdependent on each other for their continued direction and momentum.

In this chapter, only a limited understanding of the complexity, interoperability, and interdependence of the above topics has been presented. Such interdependences, when working normally, create efficiencies that are extremely difficult to compete with if one is a second- or third-world nation. It is consistency and forward progression that provides the momentum for day-to-day normality and continuity in modern societies, and as such, make them subject to greater harm when disrupted. When the underlying systems that are used by individuals, groups, organizations, and key sectors are disrupted through physical attacks, cascading psychological consequences can effectively bring an economy to its knees, if only for a few days. Killing the momentum in a society in a competitive world may be power enough for its enemies, as it provides additional time and future opportunities for continued aggression. The shear size and magnitude of such an economy in chaos may produce a reactive mindset instead of a proactive and forward thinking approach to securing ongoing operations. It is this reason that a preventative wakeup call must be heard before one is founded in reaction.

References

Belcher, T., & Yoran, E. (2002, July). *Riptech Internet security threat report. Attack trends for Q1 and Q2 2002* (Vol. 2).

Best, R. (2004, September). *The National Intelligence Director and intelligence analysis* (CRS Report for Congress).

Borjas, G. (2002, June 17). Rethinking foreign students: A question of the national interest. *National Review.*

Dam, K. (2002, September). *Testimony of Kenneth W. Dam, Deputy Secretary Department of the Treasury, before the Financial Services Committee of the United States House of Representatives. Terrorist financing: A progress report on implementation of the USA PATRIOT Act.*

Freebersyer, J., & Macker, J. (2001). Realizing the network-centric warfare vision: Network technology challenges and guidelines. *Proceedings of the IEEE Military Communications Conference.*

Futures Industry Association. (2005). *Global futures and options volume rose 8.9% in 2004.* Retrieved from http://www.futuresindustry.org/presscen-2169.asp?pr=55

Giles, L. (1910). *Sun Tzu on the art of war, The oldest military treatise in the world* (Translated from the Chinese, 1910). Retrieved from http://www.molossia.org/milacademy/suntext.html

Hepp, P., Hinostroza, E., Laval, M., & Rehbein, F. (2005). *Technology in schools: Education, ICT and the knowledge society.* Retrieved from http://www1.worldbank.org/education/pdf/ICT_report_oct04a.pdf

Hoene, C., Baldassare, M., & Brennan, C. (2002, December). *Homeland security and America's cities.* (Research Brief on America's Cities, 2002-2).

Institute for Security Technology Studies at Dartmouth College. (2002, December). *Cyber-security of the electronic power industry*. Investigative Research for Infrastructure Assurance Group.

International Telecommunication Union (ITU). (2005). *Key indicators of the telecommunication/ICT sector*. Retrieved from http://www.itu.int/ITU-D/ict/index.html

Lewis, J. (2002, December). *Assessing the risks of cyber-terrorism, cyber-war and other cyber-threats*. Center for Strategic and International Studies.

National Center for Education Statistics. (2003, October). *Internet access in U.S. public schools and classrooms: 1994-2002*. Institute of Education Sciences.

National Center for Education Statistics. (2004, June). *The condition of education 2004 in brief*. Institute of Education Sciences.

National Center for Education Statistics. (2004, December). *Digest of education statistics 2003*. Institute of Education Sciences.

National Center for Health Statistics. (2004). *Health, United States, 2004, with chartbook on trends in the health of Americans*.

National Commission on Terrorist Attacks Upon the United States. (2003, July). *Hearing of the National Commission on Terrorist Attacks Upon the United States, Public hearing, Terrorism, Al Qaeda, and the Muslim world*.

Office of Technology and Electronic Commerce (OTEC). (2005). *Research by industry/sector*. Retrieved from http://web.ita.doc.gov/ITI/itiHome.nsf/IndSectorInfo!OpenForm&Start=1&Count=999&Expand=4&Seq=3

Pearce, L. (2004, November). *Encyclopedia of American industries* (4th ed.). Thompson Gale.

Quick, A. (2002, November). *Encyclopedia of global industries* (3rd ed.). Thompson Gale.

Symantec. (2003, September). *Symantec Internet security threat report*. http://downloads.securityfocus.com/library/InternetThreatReportSept2003.pdf

Tatelman, T. (2005, January). *Intelligence Reform and Terrorism Prevention Act of 2004: National standards for drivers' licenses, social security cards, and birth certificates*. Congressional Research Service.

United States Department of Commerce. (2004). *Statistical abstract of the United States: 2003* (123rd ed.). U.S. Census Bureau.

United States General Accounting Office. (2004, March). *Challenges and efforts to secure control systems.* Retrieved from http://www.gao.gov/new.items/d04354.pdf

United States General Accounting Office. (2005). *Efforts of the financial services sector to address cyber-threats.* Subcommittee on Domestic Monetary Policy, Technology, and Economic Growth, Committee on Financial Services, House of Representatives. Retrieved from http://www.gao.gov/new.items/d03173.pdf

Zernic, M., Freudinger, L., & Morris, A. (2001, March). Aeronautical satellite assisted process for information exchange through network technology (Aero-SAPIENT) project: The Initial Trials. *Proceedings of the IEEE Aerospace Conference.*

Additional Readings

Air Land Sea Application Center. (1996, May). *TALK II-SINCGARS, Multiservice communications procedures for the single-channel ground and airborne radio system.* United States Marine Corp.

Allen, W., Fletcher, D., & Fellhoelter, K. (2005). *Securing critical information and communication infrastructures through electric power grid independence.* Retrieved from http://www.hi-availability.com/pdf/CriticalInformation.pdf

Alpert, B. (2004, May 17). Here come e-pills. *Barron's.*

Block, R., & Fields, G. (2004, October 1). Effort to create terror watch list is falling behind, report finds. *Wall Street Journal.*

Bradford, P., Brown, M., & Perdue, J. (2004). Towards proactive computer-system forensics. *Proceedings of the International Conference on Information Technology: Coding and Computing.*

Cantos et al. (2000, June). Cyber-Security Information Act introduced in the House. *Journal of Proprietary Rights, 12*(6).

Cebrowski, A. (1999, June). CNE and CAN in the network centric battlespace; Challenges for operators and lawyers. *Naval War College Symposium on Computer Network "Attack" and International Law.*

Clarke, T., DeLoria, W., & Tall, A. (1995, November). Defense message system overview. *Proceedings of the IEEE Military Communications Conference.*

Clem, A., Galwankar, S., & Buck, G. (2004, March). Health implications of cyber-terrorism. *Prehospital and Disaster Medicine, 18*(3).

Commission for Review of FBI Security Programs. (2002, March). *A review of FBI security programs.* U.S. Department of Justice.

Daalder, I. (2002, July). *Assessing the Department of Homeland Security.* The Brookings Institution.

David, M., & Sakurai, K. (2003, March). Combating cyber-terrorism: Countering cyber-terrorist advantages of surprise and anonymity. *Proceedings of the 17th International Conference on Advanced Information Networking and Applications.*

Dawson, W. (2003, April). Homeland security information sharing architecture. *National Defense Industrial Association Interoperability and Systems Integration Conference.*

Di Pietro, R., & Me, G. (2002, October). Military secure communications over public cellular network infrastructure. *Proceedings of the IEEE Military Communications Conference.*

Emerson, S. (2003, July). *Terrorism financing: Origination, organization, and prevention: Saudi Arabia, terrorist financing and the war on terror.* United States Senate Committee on Governmental Affairs.

Farrar et al. (2004, April). Wireless communications infrastructure in a military environment. *Proceedings of the IEEE Sarnoff Symposium on Advances in Wired and Wireless Communications.*

Filman, R. (2004, March/April). Air system information management. *IEEE Internet Computing.*

Franke, E. (1998). Architectural considerations for a family of multifunctional tactical intelligence terminals. *Proceedings of the IEEE Military Communications Conference.*

Friedman, N. (2002, September). *Distributed energy resources interconnection systems: Technology review and research needs.* National Renewable Energy Laboratory.

Gladis, P. (2004, November). *The application of DNE technologies TAC-300 & TAC-900 multiservice access concentrators in department of defense communications network.* Ultra Electronics.

Global Justice Information Sharing Initiative. (2004, March). *Applying security practices to justice information sharing*. Security Working Group.

Hauck et al. (2002, March). Using Coplink to analyze criminal-justice data. *Computer*.

Homjak, A., & Howard, W. (2000, May). An innovative GIS-based telecommunications infrastructure integration system for Schriever Air Force Base cable plant management. *Proceedings of the Conference on Information Systems for Enhanced Public Safety and Security*.

Institute for Security Technology Studies at Dartmouth College. (2002, December). *Cyber-security of the electric power industry*.

Jana et al. (2003, October). Empowering the battlefield with a mobile middleware platform. *Proceedings of the IEEE Military Communications Conference, 22*(1).

Jasani, H. (2002). Secure multimedia activity with redundant schemes. *Proceedings of the IEEE SoutheastCon*.

Jorgensen, E. (1999, August). *Proposed DoD guidelines for implementation of a Web-based joint IETM*. Naval Surface Warfare Center.

Kersten, D. (2005, February). Building the medical Internet. *Government Executive, 37*(2).

Krol, M. (1997, October/November). Telemedicine, A computer/communications current and future challenge. *IEEE Potentials*.

Kun, L. (2004, January/February). Technology and policy review for homeland security, The importance of our data and the need for a systems approach to information technology. *IEEE Engineering in Medicine and Biology Magazine*.

Long, D. (2000, May). Civil infrastructure dependency — The military "Achilles heel" or another facet of normal operations in the 21st century. *Proceedings of the Conference on Information Systems for Enhanced Public Safety and Security*.

Markle Foundation. (2003). *Creating a trusted network for homeland security*. Markle Foundation Task Force.

Masse, T., & Krouse, W. (2003, October). *The FBI: Past, present, and future*. Congressional Research Service, The Library of Congress.

Masson, B., & Payeur, G. (1996, October). Integrated environmental, security, power monitoring and control in telecommunication remote sites.

Proceedings of the 18th International Telecommunications Energy Conference.

McGee, M. (2004, March). E-medical records get marketing makeover. *Information Week.*

Milanovic et al. (2003, August). Distributed system for lawful interception in VOIP networks. *Proceedings of EUROCON 2003.*

National Infrastructure Protection Center. (2002, August). *Blue Cascades table top exercise.* Pacific North-West Economic Region.

National League of Cities. (2005). *Homeland security: Practical tools for local governments.* Retrieved from http://www.tisp.org/

National Research Council of the National Academies. (2005). *Cyber-security of freight information systems, A scoping study.* Transportation Research Board.

Parmenter, E. (2004). Health care benefit crisis: Cost drivers and strategic solutions. *Journal of Financial Service Professionals, 58*(4).

Ponder, R. (2004). IT is coming to a physician near you. *Health Management Technology, 25*(7).

Raymond, B. (2005). The Kaiser Permanente IT transformation. *Healthcare Financial Management, 59*(1).

Rumsfeld, D. (2004). *Annual report to the President and the Congress.*

Scalingi, P. (2001). *Critical infrastructure protection initiatives for electric power.* IEEE Power Engineering Society Winter Meeting.

Schumacher, H., & Ghosh S. (1999, October). Unifying the secure DoD network and public ATM network infrastructure. *Proceedings of the IEEE Military Communications Conference.*

Shake, T. (1999). Security in military/commercial communication gateways. *Proceedings of the IEEE Military Communications Conference.*

Simpson, G. (2000, October 18). Terror finance suspects face prison. *Wall Street Journal.*

Space and Naval Warfare Systems Command. (2000, May). *Security requirements.* Naval Information Systems Security Office.

United States Department of Defense. (1992, September). *MIL-STD-188-183, Department of Defense Interface Standard, Interoperability Standard for 25-KHZ TDMA/DAMA Terminal Waveform.*

United States Department of Defense. (1996, May). *MIL-STD-188-185, Department of Defense Interface Standard, Interoperability of UHF MILSATCOM DAMA Control System.*

United States Department of Defense. (2005). *Active duty military personnel by rank/grade.* Retrieved from http://web1.whs.osd.mil/mmid/military/RG0412.pdf

United States Department of Homeland Security. (2003, February). *The national strategy to secure cyber-space.*

United States Department of Homeland Security. (2004, June). *A report from the Task Force on State and Local Homeland Security Funding.* The Homeland Security Advisory Council.

United States Department of the Navy. (2003, January). *COMSC Instruction 3430.1.*

United States Department of Transportation. (2003, September). *Maritime Administration, Strategic plan for fiscal years 2003-2008.*

United States General Accounting Office. (GAO) (2003, January). *Critical infrastructure protection, Efforts of the financial services sector to address cyber-threats.*

United States General Accounting Office. (GAO) (2004, March). *Critical infrastructure protection, challenges and efforts to secure control systems.*

United States General Accounting Office. (GAO) (2005, April). *Information security, Internal Revenue Service needs to remedy serious weaknesses over taxpayer and Bank Secrecy Act data.*

Vogelzang, W., & Hodge, R. (1992, October). Goal architecture and transition strategy for the Defense Information System Network. *Proceedings of the IEEE Military Communications Conference.*

Chapter VII

Thoughts for
the Future

Objectives of This Chapter

√   Briefly put the previous information presented into a context for taking action.

√   Understand the relationship between user privacy and data usage.

√   Be aware of the relationship between security design and user features.

√   Present some of the major issues in securing the global information infrastructure.

√   Identify seven solutions for safeguarding the global information infrastructure from cyber criminals and cyber terrorists alike.

Introduction

In the previous chapters of this book, an examination of many of the approaches and motivations of terrorist organizations were presented, as well as their increasing use of the global information infrastructure to communicate, coordinate, and facilitate terrorist activities. The emergence of a cyber terrorist facilitating physical acts of violence in order to create widespread fear, brings with it a host of implications about the future of our electronic security. The vulnerabilities that continue to exist throughout telecommunication systems such as telephones, mobile accesses, cable, satellite, and Internet systems is blood in the water for hungry sharks of all kinds. Sectors such as public and private utilities, banking and finance, transportation, manufacturing, medical, education, and government, all use the global information infrastructure for daily operations and as such, may fall victim to these same technologies. It does not matter that the predator is a cracker, cyber criminal, or cyber terrorist when it comes to addressing corrective measures, or the underlying conditions and inherent dependencies that exist in today's global environment. Because securing the global information infrastructure involves so many stakeholders, encompassing national and international interests that are governed by individual governments throughout the world, an examination of the larger political and economic issues must be discussed in order to construct preventive, corrective, and responsive initiatives.

In a 1995 paper by Ølnes and Spilling entitled *The new European regulatory environment for telecommunications — Implications for service management and its security*, the authors offer that market-driven nation states and economic federations are governed and impacted by the following:

- **General laws**. In any new initiatives, all relevant law, trade legislation, and treaties must be followed. This includes addressing the influences that can be asserted by the regulators such as the legislature and law enforcement.

- **National security and public order**. Because the integrity and availability of a country's telecommunication infrastructure can be of critical importance, initiatives that change or alter these systems' state of readiness will require direct input from those agencies responsible for maintaining national security and public order. This also includes the application of strong encryption when the monitoring of communications traffic is enacted in the name of national security.

- **Privacy and protection of personal data**. The requirements to protect the privacy of personal data vary from country to country. These variations have their origins in the expected use of this information by various interests within each country. Any new initiatives must adhere to these requirements, or be prepared to have said requirements changed to accommodate the initiative.

- **Protection of intellectual property**. Extensive laws and treaties have established methods and measures for dealing with the theft or misuse of intellectual property within a nation's borders and internationally. These must be considered when introducing additional security measures.

- **Licensing of providers**. Because certain transmission frequencies and mediums fall under public licensure, and various countries strongly regulate certain sectors through licensing, these organizations must operate in a regulated environment. Such regulations, and any additional restrictions that are imposed, must be considered when changes are instituted for any potential impact.

- **Monitoring of fair competition**. Market-driven economies generally choose competitive forces over monopolies. This is because when there is too much influence that is derived from market dominance, price and innovation become casualties. Care must be taken in initiatives that impact market share control.

- **Standardization, equipment certification and technical regulations**. Most industries have standards by which they design, construct, and establish communication. In many cases, certain products are required to be certified to perform at a specified capacity or meet various technical regulations. The smallest change to this environment can have profound consequences to an entire industry and must be considered.

Though the paper's intent was focused around the European Union, such understandings can be applied to nearly any global effort. All of the above items apply to political and economic initiatives that are to be effective in achieving information security policy at a local, national, and international perspective. Successful initiatives to secure the global information infrastructure must include these influences or be short lived. As a subset of the above, the following section brings to light several key issues that directly impact the future consideration of security initiatives.

Key Issues to Be Considered

What is put forward by the security industry as a solution to correcting information security related issues is a combination of security mechanisms, public awareness and security training, data reporting, and onsite management assistance by vulnerability assessment and law enforcement organizations. The current state of the security industry is that it has numerous, well financed organizations making small, incremental improvements in information security, with few large leaps in success. This is because in reality, information security has become an industry that resides in the realms of politics and economics, and now is emerging into a critical national security issue. In 2004, The Yankee Group stated that the global security market will generate US$12.9 billion in revenue for 2004, and is mostly composed of threat mitigation, command and control, and managed security services. Such a number is not a very large amount when viewed as a percentage of the global gross domestic product presented in Chapter I (i.e., estimated at about US$37 trillion for 2004). This can be viewed that the global security market is either extremely efficient, or is underdeveloped and/or is an underutilized market of goods and services. Such a question is worthy of further research. None the less, economic dominance and electronic connectivity are strongly tied together (see Figure 19).

Of the top 20 Internet subscription countries, only Turkey and Argentina do not reside in the top 20 GDP countries. In this author's opinion, these top 20 countries must begin increasing their respective security initiatives by applying additional resources towards the development and/or implementation of widespread security technologies. In addition, the need to secure their infrastructures also solicits their unified, multijurisdictional cooperation in considering all of the political and economic factors presented in the previous section if a holistic security approach is to be obtained.

For most people, a key issue when using the global information infrastructure is how do you have privacy in a public space. Because people in open, democratic, market-driven systems have power through their voting and purchasing, their need and/or demand for privacy must be considered. The vulnerability of data communication systems has been with us for over a quarter century. The reality is that businesses that purport to securely store and manage private information have a long history of having their stored and transmitted information stolen whenever they are connected to larger, networked systems. This is especially true of Internet connectivity in the theft of credit card and customer details. This is primarily caused by the relationship between user

Figure 19. Top 20 Internet subscriptions vs. top 20 GDP countries (OTEC, 2005)

Internet Subscribers			Gross Domestic Product		
Rank	Country	Subscribers	Rank	Country	2002 (Billions)
1	United States	159,000,000	1	United States	9234.13
2	China	71,030,000	2	Japan	5666.83
3	Korea (South)	41,999,210	3	Germany	2708.08
4	Germany	39,000,000	4	France	1831.53
5	United Kingdom	25,000,000	5	United Kingdom	1361.09
6	Japan	23,913,363	6	Italy	1234.34
7	France	21,900,000	7	China	1207.27
8	Italy	18,500,000	8	Brazil	812.11
9	Brazil	16,718,293	9	Canada	753.41
10	Canada	16,110,000	10	Spain	738.59
11	Russia	14,000,000	11	Korea, South	680.29
12	Netherlands	11,000,000	12	India	533.66
13	Mexico	10,405,013	13	Netherlands	505.05
14	Spain	9,789,000	14	Australia	468.67
15	Poland	8,970,000	15	Russia	381.58
16	Australia	5,898,700	16	Mexico	375.43
17	Turkey	5,500,000	17	Taiwan	344.51
18	Sweden	5,125,000	18	Switzerland	339.30
19	Taiwan	4,779,000	19	Belgium	321.30
20	Argentina	4,587,000	20	Sweden	300.42

privacy (i.e., secrecy) and data usage (i.e., transparency). The issue of secrecy tends to have a political orientation that is offset by the need to have the transparency of data and information for personal and professional self-interests. The more private you make something, the less use it is to all the competing interests seeking to exploit it. While this seems to be an obvious concept, market systems tend to justify this mistreatment as a matter of competitiveness, and will therefore generally find a way to get the information and exploit it (i.e., political and economic motivations). It is the accumulation, storage, and transmission of data and information that are the beginning points of its theft. The secondary reason systems and processes are not as secure is the relationship between user features and security design. Fundamentally, the most secure system is one that is unplugged from all other systems and has little or no user features. The more flexibility that a system has for a user to interact and take greater control over it, produces greater complexity and interoperability

Figure 20. Security matrix of competing interests

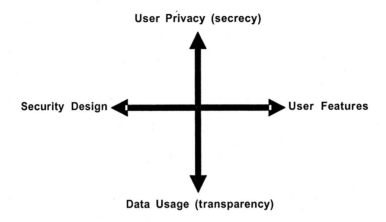

issues. These may, in turn, be exploited by those with less than honorable agendas. The more complex a system is, the more opportunities are present for unintended errors, defects, and vulnerabilities. These two continuums (i.e., privacy/data usage — user features/security design) can be unified to form a security matrix that identifies the competing interests to securing any publicly influenced system (see Figure 20).

As a result of these competing interests, security initiatives will continue to encounter strong resistance by consumers, developers, and legislators in open market economies, unless such initiatives are in their basic self-interests, and the perceived loss in any one direction is worth the perceived security gain. Therefore, something must be given in exchange for any perceived loss for an initiative to have longevity.

Another key issue at hand is the need for comprehensive security in governing systems. Reducing vulnerability in organizations requires the implementation and maintenance of security policies, periodic vulnerability assessments and corrective action, continuous awareness training, and the utilization of expertise for ongoing technical solutions and response capabilities. But it is not just the hardware, software, and storage systems that must be secured. As an initial starting point for securing all accesses, storage, and transmission of an organization's data and information, entities need to clearly identify all data and information that is nonpublic in nature as the foundation to any security approach. This includes any partner relationships with other entities that are the recipient of nonpublic data and information. The establishment of policies and procedures, with the purpose of enforcing the security of this data and information must include the periodic auditing of these policies and procedures. The main problem is that this approach does not go far enough, as ongoing penetrations by criminals have proven. There are few examples of truly "secure" systems that have not had successful attacks resulting in some loss of confidentiality, integrity, or availability. At the root of the problem is the so-called need for organizational access to data and information. While there exist the unrestricted access, collection, and storage of nonpublic data, the incentive for security breaches will continue. The above is further compounded by the lack of deployment of state-of-the-art security mechanisms in a holistic manner throughout the global information infrastructure and the components that comprise it. An example of this is, despite the fact that a large part of the military infrastructure (i.e., DoD, etc.) utilizes pathways and processing components that are used by the general public, the parts of their infrastructure that are under direct control have far greater security capabilities, combat grade components, and effective policies and procedures than its public equivalent. Therefore, one must ask why this military grade infrastructure has not been deployed through-out the rest of the public infrastructure. This author can only speculate that the users' demands or perceived requirements for security do not warrant the added costs associated with such improvements. Regardless of the reasons, it seems only rational that such capabilities should be disseminated and deployed if any serious effort to secure our infrastructures is to succeed.

The last major issue presented in this section deals with the core reasons for security breaches, and the evolutionary aspect to breaches and protective mechanisms. From the information systems security perspective, security is about protecting the confidentiality, integrity, and availability of data. This simplistic perspective is the foundation of information security, and can be viewed as the following:

- Preventing the unauthorized reading of data or messages
- Preventing the unauthorized changes of data or messages
- Preventing the delay or disruption of data or message access

In a secure system, this implies that access is granted only to an authorized party. This also implies that any data or message was sent by an authenticated individual, and that the receiver of the data or message was received by an authenticated individual, and both parties cannot deny sending, receiving, or accessing said data or message. The receipt or access of data and/or a message requires this content to be protected on whatever system it is accessed or viewed upon. These understandings are designed to counteract the following:

- The testing of individual and/or group cracking capabilities
- The testing of the defensive capabilities of an attacked entity
- To undermine a target's communications effectiveness
- The use of a cracked system for future attacks
- The access, modification, deletion, and/or theft of data or information contained within a system

These two competing understandings are engaged in an endless game of one-upmanship. As soon as one creates an innovation, the other outdoes it. It is sheer arrogance to believe that any one proposed solution can resolve security breaches, but instead, solutions must be pursued with an understanding that they may one day be defeated. It is with this understanding that the next section is written and offered to you, the reader.

Proposed Solutions

In the following sections, what will be presented is a series of prevention, response, and future policies that directly relate to the above key issues, and will hopefully help shape the current state of the information security landscape. What will not be presented in any significant depth are the well-established practices, procedures, and processes of the information security domain. There are numerous books that detail and govern the information security approach. Instead, this chapter shall attempt to propose ideas that address many of the larger issues governing the protection of data and information, and in doing so, help to mitigate the emerging threat of cyber terrorism.

Information as a Property Right

Simply put, property can be considered a possession that its owner may dispense with as they see fit, and is generally a relationship between people with regards to that possession. This means that an understanding between people as to how a possession such as information is to be governed in a civil society is clearly understood. The notion of making information a property right permits its owner certain controls of usage and just compensation for its theft or misuse. Regulators (i.e., governmental or nongovernmental) need to establish a clear delineation between public and private information in order to distinguish what information has ownership potential. Such a delineation needs to be created through a joint initiative between businesses, government, technology providers, privacy advocate groups and citizens, alike. While initially such a process may be laborious, these standards would have a prolific impact on enforcing privacy, establishing future legislative initiatives, designing storage and transmission systems, and judicial rulings, when breaches do occur.

Information designated as public data or information may be utilized by anyone with the legal right to do so (i.e., intellectual property rights). Therefore, all security requirements would become the responsibility of the owner to enforce and monitor, and as such, would become purely a civil matter when breaches do occur. That which is designated as private data or information must be secured throughout any collection, storage, usage, transmission, and deletion process. Fulfilling all security requirements would fall to the organization "leasing" the data or information, and the responsibility to prevent its misuse or theft would become the organization's responsibility. Breaches beyond the security industry's established standards would result in civil penalties, payable to those who were negatively impacted and criminal penalties for the officers of the organizations that failed to protect it. In addition, private data must have a legal shelf life as a primary measure of securing its usage and preventing its abuse. For the above to work effectively, there must not be any exemption for specific organizations (i.e., government vs. business vs. individual needs) because once one exemption is made, history has shown more shall follow.

Global Information Security Center

Another aspect of information security that must be considered on a global basis is security breaches and reporting. Currently, efforts to collect and disseminate security breaches are fragmented. While organizations such as the SANS Institute and CERT Coordination Center do a wonderful job at a regional level, data is not easily shared, or in a unified format. In this author's opinion, what is needed is the establishment of a centralized reporting structure, such as a global information security center. Such a center would create an aggregated data structure of security vulnerabilities and breaches for global reporting by regional security organizations. Such collected information by organizations would need to be universally formatted, so that it may be freely distributed and integrated between participating entities. This includes all detection and emergency response collaboration efforts. Because history has shown that governments have great difficulty remaining efficient and politically neutral, any centralization efforts must be conducted by a private organization, and may be supported in part by government funding.

Another initiative that could be assigned to such an organization is a top-down examination of the chief information vulnerabilities by sector and infrastructure technologies (i.e., SCADA systems, etc.). Along with this examination, government information collection and storage reduction standards must be re-examined to reduce the government's excessive need to collect and store data on individual citizens. This information is now being configured for intergovernmental and transgovernmental sharing initiatives, and needs to be secured with a long-term perspective. One of the easiest ways to secure this data is to not collect it to begin with. Because such data belongs to the individual citizen (i.e., providing the previous initiative occurs), a secure audit trail by government and/or agency employees who access this citizen data must be created. With the computerization of this data, such an audit trail is easily implemented. It is also suggested that individual citizens may access said audit trails in the same way as the Freedom of Information Act provides for reading ones own governmentally stored records. In this way, the misuse of government-controlled information can be pursued. Agencies and departments that cannot provide an effective audit trail must be denied sharing capabilities with other agencies and departments. As an added measure of management, civilian oversight of data mining and usage activities should be implemented. This must be composed of non-presidential appointees, unlike in the case on the National Intelligence Director's oversight board. In this way, the appointees do not share a common appointer.

Economic sectors, in turn, would follow suit, as the government is a big factor in influencing data collection by other stakeholders. It is this author's opinion, the trend of unifying intelligence through a shared set of informational networks and decentralization must, instead, be compartmentalized, as a requirement for securing critical and confidential information. Instead, an aggregation should be used for central reporting of high-priority initiatives and intelligence as a matter of importance to national security. When data and information is made available between divisions and departments in an unaggregated form, an opportunity to intercept and abuse it emerges. As part of the overhauling of government information processing, a consolidation and simplification of computer crime legislation is also required, and can be facilitated by the global information security center. Legislation, such as the Computer Fraud and Abuse Act, Electronic Communications Privacy Act, and the Stored Communications Act, and others, must clearly define the law in a simple and concise manner that focuses on the interception, access, modification, or destruction of the data and information that is stored and/or processed by computers. It must also be geared towards international collaboration for multijurisdictional operations. It is time that directives to secure our infrastructures clearly show an understanding that the information is more important than the computer it is stored or processed on, and this can be the global information security center's primary mission statement.

Alter Software Licensure Agreements

Fundamental to the software manufacturing industry is the premise that their products are not owned by the user but are, instead, licensed. The user is simply purchasing the right to use the software, and as such, must also agree to a set of terms and conditions in the licensure agreement. Because of this, software producers have been permitted to require the user to accept any and all liability derived from the software's usage, regardless of defects and incompatibilities. No warranties are expressed or implied as a result. It is only competition and the potential for legislative changes that keep most producers from releasing poorly produced or designed software. The responsibility for software defects, flaws, and vulnerability has been partially addressed through the use of updates. Regardless of intention or competency, companies that produce software and firmware should provide timely, secure updates to reported vulnerabilities of their respective products. In this way, a security product industry that is responsive to changing conditions will be able to maintain a suitable level of trust. Realistically, such product producers must be permitted to establish an expiration of support services, and this expiration should be clearly included on all packaging and ordering information. Updates to these products should also be labeled fee-based or free on said packaging and ordering information so the product's support liability is explicit. However responsive that this approach may seem, it is but a symptom of the larger problem.

Because many updates continue to address repetitive design flaws, safeguards against well-established vulnerabilities such as buffer overflows and the like must be eliminated prior to their release. The software industry must be encouraged to stop releasing products that rely on the "early deployment and then patch the product while in use" approach. In this author's opinion, the only way to do this is by eliminating the cloak of protection that is afforded through licensure agreements. Whether through legislative initiatives or judicial rulings, the deployment of software with well-established security vulnerabilities must come with a nullification of the entire licensure agreement. This single notion would radically alter the mass production of software designed and produced throughout the world.

Creation of an Underwriters Laboratory of Security Products

To begin this section, this author would like to start by stating two fundamental criticisms facing any effort to secure the global information infrastructure. The first of these is the role of security standards organizations that establish common definitions, standardized product requirements, benchmarking comparisons, and product testing. There is an implied consumer understanding that when a new security product is commercially released, a rigorous examination of its claimed features has been performed. This is especially true when a given product is claimed to be fill-in-the-blank-standard compliant. Standards, and the organizations that create and maintain these standards, are consensus-building structures comprised mostly of representatives from the commercial interests in the industry that seeks the standardization. What this means is that standards are designed for compatibility and generalities to enable the participating organizations to meet a given standard, rather than exclude any represented commercial interest from being compliant. As part of their on-going consensus-building activities, these standards organizations sponsor events such as security conferences, workshops, and the like, in order to invite outside research to propose new innovations in their particular domains. The problem is that despite continuous calls by researchers to perform destructive testing on products, and in particular the core security technologies that are the basis of the new products such as encryption algorithms, standards organizations have failed to thoroughly integrate such testing as a matter of compliance. Other industries have successfully standardized the safety requirements of introduced products through organizations such as Underwriters Laboratories (UL) and the Canadian Standards Association (CSO). Without an independent, preproduct security testing standards organization, it is this and other authors' opinion that breaches will continue to be widespread in poorly designed technologies. This is especially true regarding the widespread implementation of such technologies.

In general, security products and critical infrastructures do not undergo sufficient scrutiny by researchers, consumers, and consumer advocates. Because security system development is an evolutionary process, penetration testing and vulnerability assessment by third parties is a preferred preventative approach to assist in the closure of security weaknesses prior to an incident. While there are surety analysis labs that test hardware and software systems for vulnerabilities, many products are still released into the marketplace only to be found insecure by private citizens. There are countless examples of hackers and crackers exploring the defenses of products and/or organizations in an effort to improve security. When the results of these efforts are reported to the source organization, they are often met with disregard or criminal prosecution.

Such a proposal was made by Janczewski and Colarik in 2003 entitled *World Framework for Security Benchmark Changes,* where a series of examination steps were to be performed on new and existing products, in order to validate any security claims made by the producer. Such a process could form the basis for the creation of an "Underwriters Laboratory of Security Products" (ULSP). An organization such as a ULSP would benefit everyone in that security products would be independently tested and certified, online systems could be examined for certification, insurance rates and civil liabilities could be reduced significantly, and the establishment of national protection standards would be in place. In addition to these benefits, global hacker participation and whistleblower protections can be used to solicit the contribution of a large number of competent people. There is a need to involve interested parties outside such an organization as a means for employing their skills and capabilities. A certification/registry system may be established that allows breaches to be pursued and reported in strict confidence, and in an ethically oriented manner in order to proactively evolve security systems and close poorly managed systems. These active whistleblowers can be registered prior to such testing, and the use of keyboard-logging audit trails can be provided as proof of the intent and process of any breach. For nontechnical whistleblowers, protections can be established to permit employees and interested third parties to disclose violations, breaches, and mismanagement of data and information of any ULSP-approved product. Remember, it takes a network structure to defeat a network structure. The untapped contributions of self-interested global citizens can be effectively mobilized to defeat a small percentage of abusive criminals. When large numbers of individuals are proactively working towards security, the environment for creating harm becomes much more limited and much more responsive to new threats and challenges.

Law Enforcement Tiger Teams

The establishment of clear, law enforcement contacts and investigative centers for the reporting and resolution of information crime is essential for responsive measures and corrective action. When a computer crime occurs, which law enforcement organization do you call? The choices consist of the local police, county sheriffs, state level enforcement, or one of many federal agencies. In many cases, when a computer crime is reported to any one of these choices, the response is that the report will be forwarded to another agency or department with more specific skills focused on these types of crime for consideration. In this author's opinion, this response is primarily due to a considerable lack of skilled computer security professionals within the law enforcement ranks. Even when a computer crime is committed, jurisdictional and procedural issues can cause too large an expense to pursue the criminals unless the victim has considerable standing. In the investigative aspect of law enforcement, a consolidation and simplification of procedural access to organizational and individual data and information must be established.

One way that this can be accomplished is through the establishment of law enforcement tiger teams. A tiger team is a term used by the military to designate a group of penetration specialists that conducted security reviews of friendly installations. With regards to electronic security, such a team would have a thorough understanding of hacking and cracking techniques in order to better identify the means, methods, and perpetrators of an intrusion, in quick response to intrusions. Such a team would not have to operate in one location, but could instead be a collection of multidepartmental and multiagency professionals that operate in a virtual organizational structure.

These tiger teams could also encompass the duties and responsibilities of a cyber counterintelligence task force for addressing criminal syndicates and terrorist activities that utilize cyberspace. Through tapping into existing counterintelligence programs, tiger teams could provide antiterrorism and force protection support within cyberspace activities. It must be noted that such a force must still operate under existing law, with regards to entrapment, jurisdiction, and due process.

Create the League of Cyber Communities

At the beginning of this chapter, the top 20 GDP and top 20 Internet subscribers were presented (see Figure 20). When the total value of the top 20 GDP countries is tallied, their combined value comprises approximately 85% of the world's GDP. This constitutes considerable influence in how global communications are utilized and controlled. Because the top 20 Internet-subscribing countries also comprise approximately 80% of the world's subscribers, this fact also constitutes considerable influence in how the Internet, and its supporting systems, are utilized and controlled. If a treaty were constructed encompassing these countries that made it possible to establish global security standards and certification processes, a significant part of the global information infrastructure could be secured. As part of such a treaty, other countries not participating or adhering to such standards would then be denied access to throughput or connecting systems if their respective system did not meet certain minimum security requirements.

Elimination of the Open Handshake Protocol

While the above proposals, if instituted, would go a long way to help secure the global information infrastructure, there is one major issue that this author believes is the foundation for insecurities, and requires new thought to be developed. While conducting research for a paper a few years ago, this author was unable to find a definitive reference for the handshake protocol. What was discovered was that the handshake protocol was a simple extension of how humans quickly negotiate the means and methods of conversations. When electronic communications were first developed, this protocol was essentially imprinted as the foundational method for the negotiation between device exchanges. As the exchanges became more automated, the protocol evolved, but continued to resemble its earlier forms. All electronic communications appear to have their origins from this approach, including the previously presented security protocols in Chapter IV. Because the very foundation of all data communications has an initial open handshake between system sessions and systems, there is a propensity or momentum to continue this open approach. As a result, I believe that the open handshake approach between devices and systems must be eliminated in order to secure all communications. While such a statement has profound implications, goes against an established and entrenched industry, researching this endeavor may very well provide new lines of thought that could restructure the entire communications industry. This simplistic concept may cause the communications industry to re-examine every aspect of communication connectivity, and as such, contribute to future technologies that can be used to secure the global information infrastructure from cyber attacks.

Final Thoughts

Regardless of its form, terrorism has clear objectives. Terrorism seeks the instilment of fear through violence in civilian populations. Terrorism pursues the controlling of people's lives through force and perceived power. It wishes for dominance over people's daily lives. When this is achieved, terrorists may profit economically and/or politically in order to increase their own particular standing in the world. Through this increased standing, terrorists will impose their will upon everyone, regardless of their participation in a given so-called movement.

Currently, there is a global effort to stop terrorism. Western countries, and those governments dependent on them, are actively engaged in their attempt to eliminate many of the supporting infrastructures of terrorism. This includes regime change, and the instilment of democratic processes where none previously existed. These initiatives also include greater controls placed on the citizens within a government's respective borders. Only time will tell if such measures yield their intended objectives. In this author's opinion, regardless of ideology or intent, terrorism in its many forms will be with us for some time.

What is needed today is a sense that individually, we need to secure ourselves, and then rely on others for security. We need to collectively step up and do what we can for the greater good during these times. Only through active participation can we truly create an environment that reduces the risks of terrorism. The first step is truly seeing the danger, and then we can begin instituting changes.

The global information infrastructure is the new supply chain for terrorist organizations and criminals alike. It allows the use of network structures, provides logistical and intelligence support, and creates a new avenue to inflicting harm on humanity at a distance. Despite the security industry's best development efforts, this infrastructure remains relatively insecure to hackers, crackers, cyber criminals and cyber terrorists alike. The full deployment of existing technologies, as well as a concerted effort, is a critical step towards protecting our economic and political infrastructure. The summary proposals presented in this chapter are but the beginning points of creating a sense of ownership in helping ourselves to lead a more secure life. Not one based in fear, but instead focused on building a more secure future.

Thank you for your attention and future contributions towards securing the global information infrastructure against the emerging threat of cyber terrorism.

References

Brenner, B. (2004, November 24). *Growing demand for command-control services*. Retrieved from http://searchsecurity.techtarget.com/originalContent/0,289142,sid14_gci1028712,00.html

Cranor, L. (1999). Internet privacy. *Communications of the ACM, 42*(2).

Farn, K., Fung, A., & Lin, A. (2003, October). Recommendation of information sharing and analysis center. *Proceedings of the 37th International Conference on Security*.

Janczewski, L., & Colarik, A. (2003, May). World framework for security benchmark changes. *Security and Privacy in the Age of Uncertainty, IFIP TC11 Proceedings of the 18th International Information Security Conference*.

Nissenbaum, H. (2000, September). *Protecting privacy in an information age: The problem of privacy in public.*

Office of Technology and Electronic Commerce (OTEC). (2005). *Research by industry/sector.* Retrieved from http://web.ita.doc.gov/ITI/itiHome.nsf/IndSectorInfo!OpenForm&Start=1&Count=999&Expand=4&Seq=3

Ølnes, J., & Spilling, P. (1995, June). The new European regulatory environment for telecommunications — Implications for service management and its security. *IEEE International Conference on Communications.*

Relyea, H. (2005, July). *Privacy and civil liberties oversight board: 109th Congress proposed refinements.* Library of Congress. Retrieved from http://www.fas.org/sgp/crs/misc/RS22078.pdf

Additional Readings

Aura, T., Roe, M., & Arkko, J. (2002, December). Security of Internet location management. *Proceedings of the 18th Annual Computer Security Applications Conference.*

Bowen et al. (2000, January). Building survivable systems: An integrated approach based on intrusion detection and damage containment. *Proceedings of the 2000 DARPA Information Survivability Conference and Exposition.*

Chabrow, E. (2002, June). Data sharing key to new agency. *Information Week.*

Dick, R. (2001, September). The legal aspects of infrastructure protection. *INFOWARCON 2001.*

Goldman, K., & Valdez, E. (2004, November/December). Matchbox: Secure data sharing. *IEEE Internet Computing.*

Kargupta et al. (2003). Homeland security and privacy sensitive data mining from multiparty distributed resources. *Proceedings of the IEEE International Conference on Fuzzy Systems.*

McLean, J. (1990). Security models and information flow. *Proceedings of the IEEE Computer Society Symposium on Research in Security and Privacy.*

Palfrey, T. (2000, October). Surveillance as a response to crime in cyberspace. *Information & Communications Technology Law, 9*(3).

Parliamentary Office of Science and Technology. (2002, October). Electronic privacy. *Postnote,* (183).

Patel, A., & Ciardhuain, S. (2000, November). The impact of forensic computing on telecommunications. *IEEE Communications Magazine.*

Patterson, C., Muntz, R., & Pancake, C. (2003, April/June). Challenges in location-aware computing. *Pervasive Computing.*

Petitcolas, F., Anderson, R., & Kuhn, M. (1999, July). Information hiding— A survey. *Proceedings of the IEEE, 87*(7).

Tantono et al. (2002, November). House approves bill easing restrictions on electronic surveillance. *Intellectual Property & Technology Law Journal, 14*(11).

Thuraisingham, B. (2005, Jan-Mar). Privacy-preserving data mining: Developments and directions. *Journal of Database Management, 16*(1).

United States Department of Energy. (2005). *21 steps to improve cybersecurity of SCADA networks.* President's Critical Infrastructure Protection Board. Retrieved from http://www.ea.doe.gov/pdfs/21steps booklet.pdf

Yurcik, W. (1999). Adaptive multilayer network survivability: A unified framework for countering cyber-terrorism. *Proceedings of the Workshop on Countering Cyber-Terrorism.*

About the Author

Andrew Colarik has a thorough knowledge of the foundations, architectures, and protocols of computer and Internet fundamentals, and their associated vulnerabilities. With over 25 years experience utilizing computerized information systems, Dr. Colarik has, and continues to provide, simple step-by-step explanations of the risks businesses face, and how to protect systems from computer attacks.

Dr. Colarik was awarded a PhD in information systems (security), and is the holder of a Master in Business Administration (MIS). The combination of his credentials with over 8 years of college teaching, providing training seminars to business, legal, and law enforcement professionals, and over 8 years as an independent consultant, brings a well-balanced insight on key security issues facing organizations today.

As a researcher, author, and inventor, Dr. Colarik has been published in top-tier security conferences, authored several information security books, and is an inventor of both utility and design patents. The latest of these publications by Dr. Colarik include: *Managerial Guide for Handling Cyber-Terrorism and Information Warfare* (February 2005), *The Home Executive's Guide to Computer Security* (November 2004), *Update/Patch Management Systems: A Protocol Taxonomy with Security Implications* (August 2004), *A Secure Patch Management Authority* (2003), *World Framework for Security Benchmark Changes* (May 2003), and *An Integrity Mechanism for File Transfer in Communication Networks* (May 2002). Additional publications are currently under development as his ongoing research into the security arena continues. Throughout Dr. Colarik's career, he has taught management of information systems, database management, programming languages, multimedia communications, application software packages, and assorted business courses. He also continues to provide systems design, network administration, equipment review and selection, troubleshooting, and hands-on training of installed systems for businesses in the financial, manufacturing, and government sectors. For additional information, visit his Web site at http://www.AndrewColarik.com.

Index

A

access control 70
Advanced Research Projects Agency
        Network (ARPAnet) 36
AH (see authentication header)
al Qaeda 2
antipiracy 39
AntiTerrorism Coalition (ATC) 50
antiterrorism movement 47
antivirus software 90
API (see application program interface)
application program interface (API) 73
ARPAnet 36
ATC (see AntiTerrorism Coalition)
asynchronous transfer mode (ATM) 63
ATM (see asynchronous transfer mode)
ATV (AntiTerrorism Coalition) 50
audit logs 106
audit trails 49
auditing 72
authentication 70
authentication header (AH) 74

B

backdoor 91
banking 124
bin Laden, O. 15, 34
bombers 24

C

CA (see certificate authority)
CATV (see cable television)
cable television (CATV) 59, 64
Canadian Standards Association (CSO)
        159
car bombings 18
CATV (cable television) network 59
certificate authority (CA) 73
CGI (see common gateway interface)
chat clients 88
COM (see component object model)
commercial-off-the-shelf (COTS) products
        130
common gateway interface (CGI) 100
communication 59, 70
component object model (COM) 93
computer forensics 44

hypertext transfer protocol (HTTP) 101

W

War on Terror 12
Web browser 87
Web-enabled application 86, 89
wireless communications 96
World Wide Web (WWW) 100
worm attacks 84
worms 92
WWW (see World Wide Web)

X

X.500 standard 73
X.509 de facto standard 73
X/Open Directory Service (XDS) 73
XDS (see X/Open Directory Service)